Layman's Bible Book Commentary
Joshua, Judges, Ruth

LAYMAN'S BIBLE BOOK COMMENTARY

JOSHUA, JUDGES, RUTH

VOLUME 4

Dan G. Kent

BROADMAN PRESS
Nashville, Tennessee

4211-74

ISBN: 0-8054-1174-7

Dewey Decimal Classification: 222.2

Subject headings: BIBLE. O.T. JOSHUA//BIBLE O.T.· JUDGES//BIBLE. O.T. RUTH

Library of Congress Catalog Card Number: 79-51136

Printed in the United States of America

To Barbara, my Deborah and Ruth

Foreword

The *Layman's Bible Book Commentary* in twenty-four volumes was planned as a practical exposition of the whole Bible for lay readers and students. It is based on the conviction that the Bible speaks to every generation of believers but needs occasional reinterpretation in the light of changing language and modern experience. Following the guidance of God's Spirit, the believer finds in it the authoritative word for faith and life.

To meet the needs of lay readers, the *Commentary* is written in a popular style, and each Bible book is clearly outlined to reveal its major emphases. Although the writers are competent scholars and reverent interpreters, they have avoided critical problems and the use of original languages except where they were essential for explaining the text. They recognize the variety of literary forms in the Bible, but they have not followed documentary trails or become preoccupied with literary concerns. Their primary purpose was to show what each Bible book meant for its time and what it says to our own generation.

The Revised Standard Version of the Bible is the basic text of the *Commentary,* but writers were free to use other translations to clarify an occasional passage or sharpen its effect. To provide as much interpretation as possible in such concise books, the Bible text was not printed along with the comment.

Of the twenty-four volumes of the *Commentary,* fourteen deal with Old Testament books and ten with those in the New Testament. The volumes range in pages from 140 to 168. Four major books in the Old Testament and five in the New are treated in one volume each. Others appear in various combinations. Although the allotted space varies, each Bible book is treated as a whole to reveal its basic message with some passages getting special attention. Whatever plan of Bible study the reader may follow, this *Commentary* will be a valuable companion.

Despite the best-seller reputation of the Bible, the average survey of Bible knowledge reveals a good deal of ignorance about it and its primary meaning. Many adult church members seem to think that its study is intended for children and preachers. But some of the newer translations have been making the Bible more readable for all ages. Bible study has branched out from Sunday into other days of the week, and into neighborhoods rather than just in churches. This *Commentary* wants to meet the growing need for insight into all that the Bible has to say about God and his world and about Christ and his fellowship.

Broadman Press

Contents

JOSHUA

JUDGES

RUTH

JOSHUA

Introduction

If you had to make a list of unsung heroes of the Bible, who would you put on it? You know, people who didn't make the headlines or get the glory, even though what they did was pivotal.

I would put Samuel on my list, and Barnabas, and John the Baptist. And I would certainly include Joshua. In fact, I might list Joshua first.

Joshua was a great and godly man. He led God's people in some of their most difficult and victorious days. Yet he lingers in the historical shadows. He is merely "the man who followed Moses." He was the man who filled Moses' shoes. It's a shame.

This is why it's good for us to have a volume like this one. It gives us a chance to study a man we generally overlook. It gives us a chance to tune in on a vital time for God's people. The things we will be able to learn will be exceeded only by the challenge and inspiration that will come to us.

Let's look now at Joshua, the man and the book.

Joshua, the Book

There's a lot we don't know about the book of Joshua. We don't know who wrote it. We don't know when it was written. We don't know much about where it was written, either. We wonder how it relates to the books of the law that go before it, and to the other books of history that follow.

Evidently the Lord didn't intend for us to be certain about the answers to these questions. However, we are most confident about the most important issues: what the book teaches, and what it means. Let's focus on those issues that are primary.

The who's and the wherefore's.—This book must have been written after the death of Joshua (24:29,31). Perhaps it was written at the same time as the books of Kings, though it contains material from an earlier time. In all, the book covers a generation, the twenty-five years between Moses and the judges, from the death of Moses to the death of Joshua. It takes in the full second generation of Israelite leadership.

Jewish tradition lists Joshua as the author of this book, but hardly anyone has held to that view for years. The book itself makes no mention of an author. Some people have turned to 24:26 for help, but that verse does not say Joshua wrote this book. It only says he wrote down the covenant God made with the people.

Joshua versus Judges?—The book of Joshua falls naturally into three unequal parts. Chapters 1-12 describe the invasion of Canaan and chapters 13-22 the distribution of the newly conquered land among the twelve tribes. Chapters 23-24 report Joshua's farewell address to his people and his death. These two final chapters include the renewal of the covenant at Shechem.

As we will see later, Joshua gives one side of the story of the conquest, Judges the other. Here in Joshua we see unified, large-scale, sweeping, effective campaigns (10:40-41; 11:16-23). In Judges, especially chapter 1, the conquest is described as slow, difficult, piecemeal, and often accomplished by individual clans.

Archaeological evidence supports both scriptural accounts. Several important cities of western Palestine, such as Bethel and Lachish in the center, Debir in the south, and Hazor in the north, were destroyed in the latter third of the thirteenth century. The research of the archaeologists points to fierce attacks and complete devastation. These cities named are located in the very areas of "General" Joshua's attacks. We need to recognize, however, that the archaeological evidence is much less certain in regard to the cities of Jericho and Ai.

Archaeological records also indicate that Canaanite culture persisted at several sites, to be eliminated by the Israelites only at a later time. This is exactly what we find in Judges and also in such passages as Joshua 13:2-6; 15:13-19,63; 16:10; 17:12-18; 23:6-8,12-13. If the Canaanites had been as completely and universally exterminated as a shallow reading of Joshua would seem to indicate, it would be difficult to account for the fact that their culture and religion continued to influence Israel adversely for several generations.

So it is a case not of either-or but of both-and. We need both outlooks to complete the picture: sudden invasion and gradual occupation. We need both the overall summary of Joshua and the detailed description we find in Judges.

The onslaught Joshua describes broke the back of Canaanite resistance and enabled Israel to establish herself in the land. However, God's people were unable at that time to subdue the coastal plain, the Esdraelon (Jezreel)

Plain, or Canaanite strongholds such as Gezer and Jerusalem (Judg. 1:21).

Is Joshua among the prophets?—Joshua is the first book of the second major division of the Old Testament. It is a book of history as far as our modern Bibles are concerned. Most Christians are surprised to learn that this book was not in the history section of the Hebrew Bible. There's a good reason for that. *There was no history section!* Joshua was in a section called Former Prophets.

Is Joshua among the prophets? To Jewish people, yes. The books of Joshua, Judges, Samuel, and Kings were Former Prophets.

How can this be? Joshua is obviously a historical record.

There is a good answer. Joshua is history, but it is history with a message. It gives history a prophetic interpretation. It was written from a prophetic viewpoint. It doesn't report dusty facts; it preaches. It has a point to get across. The author selected and presented the facts that would glorify God and bring people to know and do his will. Like all Bible historians, he was interested in the effects of the facts.

Promises fulfilled . . . if . . . .—The book of Joshua centers on the fulfillment of God's promises, particularly the promise of the land. God had promised the land to the patriarchs and to Moses. Joshua tells us how that promise was finally fulfilled.

The message of Joshua is that the Chosen Land was to be theirs, but only on one important condition: obedience to the Law God had given through Moses (1:7-8). This is the theme of Deuteronomy, carried over directly into Joshua. This is why Joshua is often called the first book of the Deuteronomic history (Joshua—Kings, history from a Deuteronomic viewpoint).

> Loyalty to God = victory and prosperity
>
> Disloyalty to God = failure and destruction

Continued well-being for the nation depended on obedience to God. Joshua and the books that follow illustrate this principle from history. Joshua is also the beginning of the long story of Israel in her national home-land.

This book reminds us that God is holy and jealous. He tolerates the worship of no other gods. Also, this God who acts in history (24:2-13) had called Israel into being as a nation. He had guided her at every step of her journey. He had given her the land. It was to be taken not by Israel's weapons but by the might of the Lord (24:12). The much land remaining to be taken was included in God's promise, according to Joshua. If Israel proved faithful, it would all be possessed and enjoyed. Because of this graciousness, Israel should love God and serve him (23:11; 24:14). Unwavering loyalty to God was the only path to national safety and prosperity (22:5).

Joshua, the Man

The president of a Baptist university was introducing the new football coach to an interested group of men. He spoke of his high hopes that the new coach would revive the sagging football program. He even spoke of a possible conference championship under the new leader. He compared him to a Moses hired to lead the school into the Promised Land.

Later someone reminded him that Moses did not lead the children of Israel into Canaan—Joshua did. (By the way, the highly-touted coach turned out to be more like Moses. One of his successors became the school's Joshua.)

Do you see how we tend to shortchange Joshua?

But even his name ought to make us sit up and take notice. Its Hebrew variations are Hoshea (Num. 13:16) and Hosea. Its New Testament equivalent is Jesus. Joshua, too, turned out to be a deliverer (savior) of his people.

Joshua was born in Egypt during the period of slavery. He was of the tribe of Ephraim. He first appeared during the battle with the Amalekites. He was Moses' general who led the troops in the fighting while Aaron and Hur held up Moses' hands (Ex. 17:8-13).

Joshua was Moses' servant (Ex. 24:13). He was on the mountain when Moses received the Law (Ex. 32:17). He was one of the twelve spies who went in to reconnoiter Canaan. Only he and Caleb returned with a positive report (Num. 14:28-30,38).

God selected Joshua to be Moses' successor long before Moses' death (Num. 27:15-28; Deut. 31:14-15,23; 34:9). When Moses died, Joshua took over without a hitch. That has to be important, because it was such a significant change.

Joshua was a military, political, and spiritual leader. He was a battlefield genius, a capable administrator for the nation, and a spokesman for God. He reminds us of some of the judges, of Saul's noble son Jonathan, or even of David as a young man.

He was at Israel's helm during the conquest and the distribution and settlement of Canaan. He led in the covenant renewal at Shechem during the last days of his life. He left his people with a stirring challenge to follow God according to the example he had set. His pattern is a hard one to better.

God had given the people the land, yes, but they still had to take it and make it their own. It was under the man Joshua that this was done (Deut. 1:38).

Joshua, the Times

The historical setting is always important when we are trying to understand the Bible. This is especially true of a book of the historical importance of Joshua. God is the Lord of history. He is a God who works out his purposes in history. He chose to reveal himself by his actions on the stage of history.

The date of the conquest.—We have already admitted that we know little about when Joshua was written. We can be a lot more certain about when the events of the book took place: the last third of the thirteenth century BC.

We have mentioned that the archaeological evidence points to a major incursion into Canaan in the thirteenth century. The fall of Lachish (Josh. 10:31-32), for instance, can be dated precisely, between 1231 and 1220. Every site so far excavated was destroyed one or more times during the period of Joshua and Judges.

The people of Israel had been prepared and disciplined by their years in the desert. They had become consolidated and hardened. They were ready for their three-phased invasion of the land: the central area, chapters 6—9; the south, chapter 10; and the north, chapter 11. Joshua's strategy was to divide the land in two and then deal with it a section at a time.

The enemy.—The Canaanites, like the Israelites, were a Semitic people. They lived mainly in the valleys and coastal areas, because water was more plentiful there and farming was easier. This meant that the hill country, the geographical backbone of Palestine, was only lightly settled. The hill country tended to be the home of isolated, dispossessed people, who would more likely be the allies of the Israelites than their opponents (9:3-15). We have already hinted that the Israelites tended to move into these areas of the central highlands.

The broken terrain of Canaan discouraged the establishment of a strong central government there. The Canaanites remained in walled city-states surrounded by satellite cities and villages, but still basically isolated. Their society was almost feudal in character. On one hand, they were strong foes because of their chariots and other heavy military equipment; on the other, they were weak because of their lack of unity and cooperation.

Egypt had long been in nominal control of Canaan. However, the pattern of this control fluctuated considerably. For the two hundred years before the conquest, Egypt's administration was a sorry pattern of oppression and corruption. Local Canaanite rulers paid tribute to Egypt and supplied workers for Egyptian construction projects. Pharaoh's troops policed Canaan but also exploited the people. The officials in charge were inefficient and dishonest. Canaanite life in general was on the decline, morale was low, and the "kings" of the city-states were weak.

The Canaanites had highly developed religion. They had an elaborate priesthood. They had many temples and shrines, all of them peopled with idols. There was also a highly-organized pantheon of gods, like the ones in Egypt, Babylonia, and Greece in the days of Homer. Their main god was Baal, the storm-god. He was also considered to be the lord of the gods and the creator of mankind.

Joshua, the Moral Questions

Our final introductory word is about the moral problems the book raises. They are too prominent and too troubling to be ignored.

The actions of Joshua and the people he led fall far below the teachings of Christ and the New Testament. We do not have much about loving your enemy or turning the other cheek here, or about doing good to those who oppose you. Rather, we have the direct, personal, complete, and brutal destruction of the foe (6:21).

We begin by admitting that Joshua lived long centuries before Christ appeared to fully and completely reveal the Father's nature and will. We should not expect completed Christian truth in a pre-Christian book.

It is clear throughout the Old Testament that the Israelites saw poison in the paganism around them, and in pagan people. Pagan religious views were a spiritual infection, deadly and highly contagious, and controlled only by strict quarantine and eradication. There is probably also in the conquest the element of God's judgment on the Canaanites for their sins.

The other side of the coin is that the Israelites received into their fellowship those native peoples who professed their allegiance to God (Rahab in 2:8-13) or desired peaceful association with them (the Gibeonites in 9:3-15).

Remember also that while Joshua is a story of holy war, such a war was probably a necessary evil. Without its wars of conquest, how could Israel have ever entered her Land of Promise or begun to realize her destiny?

The Conquest of Canaan

(1:1 to 12:24)

Preparation for the Invasion (1:1 to 5:15)

The book of Joshua takes up where the book of Deuteronomy leaves off. It is a continuation of the same account. Chapter 1:1-2 reminds us that Moses had died, as Deuteronomy 34:5 says. Joshua was his duly selected and duly anointed successor (Josh. 1:1), as Deuteronomy 34:9 and many previous passages indicate. The first verses of one book and the last verses of the other do much to tie the two documents together.

Joshua does take a brief backward glance, but, of course, the story moves on from there. The first several chapters deal with getting ready to actually enter the land.

The Summons to the Task (1:1-18)

Both Joshua and the people had been assigned responsibilities years before. Now, however, the theory was giving way to practice. What had been only prospect for so many years was about to become reality. The Lord took the occasion to challenge both leader and people with what lay ahead of them.

God's summons to Joshua (1:1-9).—The death of Moses had apparently just occurred. Perhaps the idea is that the prescribed thirty days of mourning had just come to an end (Deut. 34:8). The title the Lord gave Moses is significant: "The servant of the Lord" (Josh. 1:1). It is a title far beyond anything man can bestow. The most important thing about Moses was his loyal obedience to God's will.

God was the only ruler his people had; so the highest possible rank for man was to be his servant. The idea of servant indicated faithful obedience to the covenant relationship and faithful leadership of the covenant people.

The great Moses was gone, but the Lord was not bereft of capable workers. He was able to turn to a younger man who had the qualifications needed for the new challenges. Joshua had often been called Moses' assistant, his lieutenant (Ex. 24:13; 33:11; Num. 11:28). Now, by inference, he was promoted to God's servant (see 24:29).

A significant change of leadership is always a pivotal time for people. This is especially true when the former leader is a giant among men, as Moses was, when the successor is completely different in personality, as Joshua was, or when the general public perceives their two leaders differently. The people of Israel deserve credit for responding so positively to Joshua's leadership. In fact, at times it seems as if they were much more ready to follow him than they had been to follow Moses. But of course the rebellious generation had died in the wilderness. This was a new generation with a new leader.

We can see three important elements in the Lord's commission to Joshua: the time has come for the promises to be fulfilled (1:2-4); you will be victorious in your every undertaking (1:5-6); you must, however, be careful to keep the law (1:7-9).

Moses is gone, the Lord reminded Joshua, and so is the generation that gave him so much trouble. The time has come for you to lead the people in going forth to claim my promises.

Verse 4 sketches a general outline of the land that lay before them. "The wilderness" means the desert region to the south and east of Canaan. "This Lebanon" indicates the high mountain ranges on the north. Mount Hermon was the highest peak in one of these ranges. The great Euphrates River lay far to the northeast. "The land of the Hittites" refers to northern Syria, which was then under Hittite control. "The Great Sea" was, of course, the mighty Mediterranean, the western boundary of the land.

It was not until David extended his empire to its farthest reaches that this description approached realization. David was able to expand his influence widely over areas he did not actually incorporate into his realm.

In verses 5-6 God assured Joshua that he would win the game, and they hadn't had the kickoff or even the opening coin toss. The Lord said that no one would be able to stand before Joshua. God gave Joshua a promise that was all any person could ask for: He would be with Joshua in the same way he had been with Moses.

The ideas of verse 6 are repeated in verses 7,9, and 18. This is a good verse to memorize. God urged Joshua to have the courage to lead Israel into Canaan.

The rest of the section, verses 7-9, returns to the theme of conditional fulfillment already seen in Deuteronomy and Joshua. All of God's help and blessings will be theirs if, *if*, IF they were faithful to God and obedient to his instructions.

Be careful, the Lord warned Joshua. Take serious care to do as Moses commanded you in the law. Don't waver. Don't get sidetracked. Follow the straight and narrow path. Don't turn aside either to the right or to the left. If you do this you will be behaving yourself wisely and prudently (this seems to be the idea of the expression "good success").

God reminded his servant that he had given the law through Moses. Here is another indication of the influence of Deuteronomy on this book. He also told Joshua what he needed to do regarding the law: Remember it, teach it, meditate on it, and do it (v. 8). In essence, God said: Don't forget my commandments; Don't stop talking of them with your mouth; Meditate on this law both day and night; Keep it ever with you, in your mind and heart, as an actual part of you; Especially take care to be obedient. Also, the ideas of prosperity and good success are repeated.

Verse 9 is a summary verse for the section. We might paraphrase verse 9 this way: "Let me say it to you again: Be strong, be courageous, don't be afraid and don't be dismayed." Why? Because Joshua was so capable and because the work before him was so easy? Not at all. Rather, because "the Lord your God is with you wherever you go."

Can't you see why, after this encounter with God, Joshua was ready to shoulder any responsibility and face any foe? He had received his divine commission for his task.

Joshua's summons to the people (1:10-18).—As soon as he had his commission from the Lord, Joshua turned to give the leader's summons to the people. He communicated with these who were to follow him by means of his subordinate officers. They received Joshua's instructions and passed them on to the people (1:10).

Joshua's adjutants or staff officers told the people to prepare rations for the actual crossing of the Jordan. Joshua informed them that the momentous event would take place in no more than three days. This would be the first step in rising up to take possession of the land the Lord had given (1:11).

There was one potential problem Joshua felt he had to be careful to head off. It involved the people of the tribes of Reuben and Gad, and the eastern section of Manasseh (1:12).

These are the groups that had earlier approached Moses with the request for fertile pastureland east of the Jordan River (Num. 32:1-42; Deut.

3:12-20). Moses had granted their petition following the defeat of the Amorite kingdoms of Sihon and Og. However, Moses had placed on them an important condition: They had to be faithful to their brothers. They had to send their troops across the Jordan with the other eight and one-half tribes and fight with them to subdue the land. The fact that their territorial claims had already been possessed could not become an excuse for them to stay at home and rest on early victories.

Joshua reminded the two and one-half tribes of Moses' command to them. He recognized that the Lord had provided them with their place of rest. Everyone agreed that it would be proper for them to leave their wives, children, and flocks and herds behind, certainly with limited military protection. Verse 14 is written from the standpoint of western Palestine. We call "Beyond the Jordan" Transjordan as opposed to Cisjordan, on the eastern side.

The soldiers of Reuben, Gad, and East Manasseh were to fight beside their brothers until the Lord gave them rest, too—until they also had taken possession of their Promised Land. Then the two and one-half tribes could return home for permanent settlement. In fact, they were not only to participate fully in the fighting, they were to serve as the point of the attack. Verse 14 says "you shall pass over armed before your brethren." These fighting men, in full battle array, were to lead the assault.

The eastern tribes had always had the proper spirit about their responsibility and continued to have it. They pledged to Joshua, as they had to Moses, to keep the agreement to the letter and even to place themselves at his disposal above and beyond the normal call of duty (1:16). They also offered a rather severe endorsement of Joshua's authority. Anyone who might be tempted to rebellion or disobedience would be executed.

These tribes pledged obedience to Joshua, as they had given it to Moses. Their only possible reservation, or implied reservation, was their insistence that Joshua had to be a leader led of the Lord as Moses had been (1:17). We see here the Hebrew resolve—true of this period of their national life at least—that their leaders be people under divine guidance.

The housekeeping details had been completed. The summonses to Joshua and to the people had been duly given and received. The stage was set for action.

On Reconnaissance in Canaan (2:1-24)

While the people were preparing for the crossing of the river, Joshua sent two spies into Canaan, into the nearby city of Jericho. Like the twelve spies from Numbers 13, these men were to reconnoiter the immediate area, its fortifications, and its general strength. Why did Joshua send only two spies? Maybe he wanted to ensure that this time there would be no minority report.

The spies hidden by Rahab (2:1-7).—The Israelite camp was at Shittim. It was the last encampment ordered by Moses before his death, and the last one mentioned in the Pentateuch (Num. 25:1). Numbers 33:49 calls this site Abel-shittim, Stream of the Acacia Trees. It was situated on the plains of Moab, the lowland territory of Moab, at the foot of the ridge across the Jordan Valley from Jericho.

Jericho was the only important city in the southern end of the Jordan Valley. It was a town of some six acres in area, five miles west of the Jordan River. This was a strategic location. It dominated the access routes that led from the lower Jordan Valley up into the highlands of Judea. Israel had to take Jericho to be able to safely advance into the central hill country. Jericho thus became the first stage of Joshua's strategy of cutting Canaan in two at the midsection.

When they reached Jericho, the two spies went to the house of a prostitute named Rahab. There were some good reasons for doing so. Living in an Oriental community was like living in a fishbowl. It was almost impossible for strangers to come and go without being noticed. Since word of whatever was going on always seemed to get around, there would be fewer questions asked about foreigners visiting such an establishment.

Strangers could expect a welcome at Rahab's house. She was in a position to be well acquainted with what was going on in the city. And, because of her status, she was probably not one of the most loyal of the local citizens.

Despite all the precautions, the king of Jericho found out about the presence of the spies. "King" is the technical term the book of Joshua uses for political officials like this, but "Kinglet" might be more appropriate. This king ruled only Jericho and a few square miles around it. He and those like him were more like princes and primarily vassals of Egypt.

The king ordered Rahab to turn over her visitors. Verse 2 says that somehow he had found out they were Israelites, and verse 3 adds the information that he knew that their mission was espionage.

Rahab, however, had hidden the two agents. She did admit to the city officials that they had visited her. However, she denied knowing where they had come from. What is more, she claimed that they had left her house about sundown, the time when the city gate was normally closed (2:4-5).

Then this brave, clever, and resourceful woman sent the searchers on a wild goose chase. She implied that the spies had escaped from the city and that only haste would make possible their capture. Like Keystone Kops, the Jericho police rushed off toward the Jordan, in the general direction of the Israelite camp. The river there was deep and swift, and could be crossed only at certain fords (2:7).

The truth was that Rahab had hidden the two spies on the roof of her house, under stalks of flax. This makes us think that these events occurred in the early spring. March was the time of the flax harvest in Canaan. The stalks, some two or three feet high, were cut and spread out on the flat roofs of the houses, where they could dry in the sun.

In this way Rahab saved the lives of the strangers.

Rahab's plea for deliverance (2:8-14).—There was method in Rahab's madness. She had a greater purpose in mind than just protecting the spies or frustrating their pursuers. She had in mind protection for herself and her family.

As she was hiding the men, she provided them with some of the intelligence information they had slipped into Jericho to obtain. She expressed her conviction that the Lord had given the Israelites the land. She admitted that fear of the invaders had fallen upon all of her people.

It was inevitable that the people of Jericho would know about the presence of the large and threatening invasion force just across the river. This was why Jericho's king was on the alert. What is more, the people of the land knew of the victories the Lord had already given his people. Good (and bad) news always travels fast, doesn't it? They knew of the crossing of the sea just after the Exodus from Egypt (Ex. 14:21-22). They knew of the defeat of the two Amorite kings in Transjordan, Sihon, and Og (Num. 21:21-35; Deut. 2:24 to 3:11). Amorites were a Semitic people. They had moved into Syria and Palestine from the northwest at the end of the Early Bronze Age. They were the major element in the population of the hill country of Transjordan. The rulers Rahab mentioned had been utterly destroyed by the Israelites. "Utterly destroyed" is a reference to holy war. It means "put under the ban" or "devoted to destruction." We'll talk more about this when we get to 6:17 and the placing of the taboo on the entire city of Jericho.

What they had heard made the people's hearts melt, Rahab said. No spirit was left in anyone. The people had begun to faint from panic (see Deut. 2:25; 11:25). It is the old story of people going to pieces over what *might* happen even though it *hasn't* yet.

The last part of verse 11 is Rahab's confession. She recognized the supremacy of Israel's God. She called him the God of all heaven and earth. She had apparently become convinced of this because of what God had already done, because of how he had already acted in history.

In later years Rahab became a prominent figure in both Judaism and Christianity. She was an ancestress of David and Jesus (Matt. 1:5). Hebrews 11:31 enrolls Rahab as a heroine of the faith, one of only two women on that list. James 2:25 mentions her, too, and says that her faith expressed itself in works.

The rest of this section describes the oath the spies exchanged with Rahab. They swore to her by the Lord that the people of Israel would deal kindly or loyally with her and with her father's house. The "sure sign" she asked for in verse 12 was evidently the solemn oath they gave. The agreement involved the sparing of Rahab's parents, brothers, sisters, and other relatives when the destruction of the city actually took place.

For their part, the two men pledged "Our life for yours!" (v. 14), their assurance that the agreement would be kept. However, they did add the condition that she continue to keep their secret. In that case, they and their people would continue to be loyal to her when the Lord actually gave them the land.

The escape of the spies (2:15-24).—The gate of the city had been closed when the Canaanite search party moved out toward the Jordan (v. 7). But the location of Rahab's house made it still possible for her to ensure the spies' escape. Because of the scarcity of space inside the town, houses were built right up to and even upon the walls.

Very little of the city of Jericho of this period has been studied by the archaeologists. Erosion and careless early excavations destroyed most of the remains from that time. However, the last Canaanite city of Jericho was surrounded by a double wall, built with twelve to fifteen feet between walls. The inner wall, of course, was the stronger of the two. Houses were built over the gap between these two walls. They rested on beams laid from wall to wall, or on small cross walls of brick.

Rahab's window evidently looked right out over the outer wall. She let the spies down to safety by means of a rope and advised them to turn west toward the hills.

As they parted, Rahab and the spies restated and reinforced their agreement. They reminded her that they would be released from responsibility if she did not live up to her part of the bargain. They cautioned her at three points. When the attack began, she was to hang a scarlet cord in the window they had escaped through. This would alert the Israelites to the location of her house. It was also a sign of faith, like the blood on the door facings of the Israelite houses during the tenth plague.

She was also to keep all the members of her family indoors during the battle. If anyone went into the street, he would be responsible for his own death, and the spies would be guiltless. If all stayed in the house as instructed and anything happened to them, the spies would be responsible.

Once again they bound her to secrecy. If she gave them away the agreement would be broken. She would be responsible for what happened, not they. Rahab agreed in full with their stipulations and even began to carry them out by binding a scarlet cord in the window. Then she sent them away. In this way one family that had no part in the Exodus took steps toward becoming a part of the covenant community. This is yet another biblical example that Israelite society was inclusive, not exclusive.

The spies escaped into the hills to the west while the authorities were searching for them along the river to the east. They hid out there in the hills until their pursuers returned, empty-handed, to Jericho. Then the spies made their way back to Joshua at Shittim and made their report. The summary in verse 24 includes the assurance that the Lord had indeed given all the land into their hands, largely because the defenders were so demoralized with fear. The city of Jericho and even the entire land was ripe for attack. Their mission of reconnaissance had been well-begun, well-conducted, and successful. Everything was ready for the actual crossing of the river.

The Crossing of the Jordan (3:1 to 5:1)

You can sense the excitement as soon as you begin to read chapter 3. The time had come to actually enter the land. Imagine the thrill of anticipation in the hearts of all the people.

Instructions for the crossing (3:1-13).—The time had come, at long last, to leave Shittim behind. And so it was that one day Joshua led the people to break camp and move to a ford of the Jordan River. After three days Joshua sent his officers throughout the camp with instructions for the people. Something new and dramatic was at hand, and new and dramatic steps had to be taken to prepare for it.

The officers told the people about the order of crossing. They were to look for the ark of the covenant. It was to be their ensign and their signal. When the ark moved they were to form their ranks and follow behind it.

The ark was carried by the Levitical priests, priests who were descendants of Levi. It was a chest, overlaid with gold and topped with cherubim on a lid of solid gold. It was portable, carried by the priests by means of rings and poles. It was hollow, and contained the tablets of the law, Aaron's rod that had budded, and a pot of manna.

Most important of all, the ark symbolized God's presence. God was thought to be invisibly enthroned above the cherubim. On the top of the ark was a gold lid known as the mercy seat. The Jews believed the mercy seat was where God met with his people. The ark usually sat in the innermost chamber of the tabernacle, the holy of holies. It was usually located in the middle of the camp. The fact that it was moving to the unusual position of the front of the procession indicated that God was not only with his people but going before them, giving them the victory, and giving them the land as he had so often promised.

Across the river was the challenge and danger of the unknown. The people were dependent on God for direction. The ark was to lead them in the way they should go (3:4). Nevertheless, they were not to follow it too closely. The ark was holy and represented the presence of the holy God. It was perilous for an unauthorized person, a layman, to get too close to the ark. The people were cautioned to stay 2,000 cubits (3,000 feet) behind the awesome presence of the Lord.

The entire account of the crossing of the Jordan is one of religious ceremony. Crossing the river was an act of faith. Even a military advance was an act of worship and of religious service. This is why Joshua instructed the people to purify themselves ceremonially in preparation for the wonders the Lord would work among them the next day. We also have the prominent involvement of the ark, representing God's presence, and the solemn procession. Crossing the river was a spiritual experience from start to finish.

Following Joshua's message to the people and the priests, the Lord spoke to Joshua: "This day I will begin to exalt you in the sight of all Israel" (3:7). What the Lord was about to do would convince the people that God was with Joshua at the crossing of the Jordan just as he had been with Moses at the crossing of the sea. God was continuing to authenticate his servant's commission.

Verse 8 is the Lord's revelation to Joshua of the remarkable thing he was about to do. The priests were to carry the ark to the brink of the water. The people would be able to cross, while the priests stood still in the Jordan.

Joshua spoke again to the people. He called them together to hear the word from the Lord. He told them how they would know for sure that the living God was among them. He told them how they would know for sure that their living God would drive out their enemies before them. The extraordinary deeds of God would give them all the evidence they would need.

Seven groups of inhabitants of Canaan are listed in verse 10. Two of them were the major elements of the population of the land, the Canaanites and the Amorites. Since both were Semitic peoples, they were related to each other ethnically and linguistically. The book of Genesis applies both names to the inhabitants of the land. The terms seem to be used interchangeably on occasions. However, Numbers 13:29 and Joshua 5:1 place the Amorites in the hill country and the Canaanites along the coastal plain and the Jordan Valley, plus the Esdraelon (Jezreel) Valley.

The other five peoples are more obscure and less important. They were non-Semitic. All were located in the hill country, except the Girgashites who are not associated with any specific region and are of unknown ethnic background. The Hivites were probably Horites (Hurrians). They originated in the kingdom of Mitanni in northern Mesopotamia and scattered out from there.

The Perizzites may have also been Hurrians, or they may have been people who lived in open villages rather than walled towns. Hittites peopled a great contemporary empire in the area of modern Turkey. Their control extended as far as northern Syria. This reference is probably to this latter area, or it may refer generally to non-Semitic people from areas north of Canaan. The Jebusites were the inhabitants of Jerusalem and are of uncertain ethnic background.

As Joshua continued to address the people, he hinted at the setting up of the memorial stones (4:1-10; see 3:12). He promised that the priests bearing the ark would lead the people across the Jordan. When their feet touched the water, the waters of the river would be stopped from flowing, and the water coming down from above would stand up in a heap.

So the people knew about the order of march, they knew what was going to happen, and they knew what their positions and responsibilities were. They were ready to move out.

The waters of the Jordan stopped (3:14-17).—At long last Joshua gave the order to move out. The people left their tents and moved toward the river in prearranged order. The priests carrying the ark of the covenant went before them. And sure enough, when the priests stepped into the water, the flow of the mighty river stopped and the people were able to pass over in safety. The priests who had been leading the procession held their position during the entire crossing. They stood on firm footing in the middle of the riverbed until all of the people had crossed.

Verse 15 adds a detail to the story that makes the miracle of the stopping of the waters even more notable. As we saw in chapter 2, the entrance into the land took place in the spring, during the harvest season for that subtropical region—probably in April. The river was swollen by spring rains and by the melting of the snows on the Lebanon Mountains far to the north. So the Jordan at that time was not just flowing, it was flooding. There were no bridges and few fords, perhaps none at that particular season of the year.

Verse 16 gives us some clues as to how the Lord may have wrought this remarkable work. It says that the waters coming down from upstream rose up in a heap at Adam. The terminology is exactly what you would expect for waters that had been caught behind a dam. However, we are not told how the water "rose up in a heap."

Adam is sixteen miles up the river from Jericho, near where the Jabbok runs into the Jordan. Zarethan is harder to identify, but it must have been some few miles further north. The sea of the Arabah, the Salt Sea, is, of course, the Dead Sea.

We can see it in this entire chapter. Without a doubt, the crossing of the river was the work not of the people but of God. It was God's action, not their achievement. It would be the same way with the conquest of the land.

The crossing completed and memorialized (4:1 to 5:1).—I know people who testify to a fascination for this chapter of Joshua that goes all the way back to childhood. That fact in itself is intriguing, because one of the purposes for these unusual happenings was the teaching of the children of future generations.

The emphasis on remembering has always been a part of both the Jewish and Christian religions. The children must always be taught what the Lord has done for us, and what he expects of us. And, of course, if the adults keep reminding the children, they will remember, too.

Chapter 4 begins with the Lord's instruction to Joshua to select twelve men, one from each of the twelve tribes. Joshua was to command each man to take a stone from the riverbed, from the very place where the priests bearing the ark were standing. They were to carry the stones with them to the place of the next encampment, which we later learn was Gilgal.

Setting up memorial stones was a common Old Testament practice. It was like our putting up a plaque or historical marker. Jacob did this with the stone that had been his pillow at Bethel (Gen. 28:18-22). He and Laban set up a stone pillar and a heap of stones to witness to their agreement at Mizpah (Gen. 31:45-52). Samuel set up the famous Ebenezer stone (1 Sam. 7:12). It memorialized the Lord's help given against the Philistines.

We see the same practice in Joshua. Stones were placed over the remains of Achan (7:25-26) and the king of Ai (8:29). At the conclusion of the great covenant renewal ceremony at Shechem, Joshua set up a large stone under the oak in the sanctuary of the Lord. He called the stone a witness to the nation's agreement with the Lord (24:26-27).

Joshua selected the twelve representative men and gave them their unusual instructions. Joshua added that what they did would constitute a sign. In later years, when their children asked "What do these stones mean to you?" (v. 6), they would have a perfect chance to teach their youngsters important spiritual truths. They would have a natural and ready-made opportunity to rehearse the mighty acts of God. We find the same situation with the Passover observance (Ex. 12:26; 13:14) and the law (Deut. 6:20).

When such occasions arise, Joshua said, "You shall tell them that the waters of the Jordan were cut off before the ark of the covenant of the Lord" (v. 7). Tell them how the waters of the swollen river were stopped, from the very moment the priests stepped in. Tell them how the priests stood in the middle of the riverbed until all the people were able to go across. Tell them how God used mighty acts to work his will, carry out his purposes, and fulfill his promises. So, Joshua said, the stones were to remind them of the miracle (4:7).

The twelve men representing the twelve tribes did as Joshua commanded them. They took up twelve stones, also representing the twelve tribes, from the middle of the riverbed. They carried them up the bank and on to the camp.

Up to now, if we hadn't read the story beforehand, we would have our minds fixed on only one set of memorial stones (3:12; 4:3,5,8). But actually there were two. Verse 9 says that Joshua set what was apparently a second set of twelve stones in the middle of the riverbed, at the place where the priests carrying the ark of the covenant were standing. And the writer adds the note that "they are there to this day." When this book was put in its final form, the pile of stones in the middle of the river was still visible at that ford of the Jordan when the water was low.

We have already said that the priests continued to stand in the middle of the streambed until the instructions regarding the memorial stones had been carried out and the people had completed their crossing (v. 10). It is interesting to note, also in verse 10, that the people crossed over in haste. They were in the presence of a miraculous work of the Lord, and they must have had confidence in his power, but they were also uncertain and perhaps even fearful. They did not know when the river would be released and the waters would surge forward again.

Then, when all the people had finished crossing over, the priests and the ark passed over before the people. This may mean that the priests left their station "in the presence of the people" (v. 11, KJV). More probably it means that the priests once again took their place at the head of the procession.

Verses 12-13 take us back to the two and one-half tribes from Transjordan. The armed men from Reuben, Gad, and East Manasseh were not encumbered by baggage or family. They had left these on the eastern side of the Jordan, where their tribal allotments were located. Thus they took their place at the head of the march, just as both Moses and Joshua had instructed (see 1:14). The plains of Jericho (v. 13) consisted of the broad area of the main Jordan Valley between Jericho and the river.

The number of warriors from the three tribes was 40,000. The word translated "thousand" here and in other places (Judg. 6:15) has the idea of "clan" or "family group." So we may well be talking about forty fighting units or forty family units.

All of these events served to exalt Joshua in the eyes of the people he was commissioned to lead. The Lord used the mighty works he had done to provide further authentication of Joshua as his chosen and capable servant. The people grew in their awe of him, just as they had stood in awe of Moses earlier. This attitude toward Joshua lasted for all of his life (v. 14).

In verse 15 the story switches back to the priests' exit from the riverbed. At the Lord's bidding, Joshua commanded them to come up from their station. When they did, the miracle of the crossing was completed. When the soles of their feet were lifted out of the mud of the riverbed, the waters returned to their place and surged again as they had before. Once again we have a miracle of perfect timing that can be explained only by the presence of God as symbolized by the ark.

Verse 19 gives us a third check on the time of year when these events took place, "the tenth day of the first month." What came to be the first month of the Hebrew calendar was the month of Abib, later called Nisan. It corresponds to our March-April. The tenth day of that month would be around the first of April, corresponding to what we found earlier in 2:6 and 3:15.

Also in verse 19 Gilgal is named as the site of the first encampment in the land. One meaning of the name is "circle." The name may refer to a circle of standing stones related to an ancient sanctuary.

Gilgal is one and one-quarter miles east of Canaanite Jericho. It was first occupied around 1200 BC or perhaps even a little earlier. For some 600 years it was both a military and a religious center. Some students of the Old Testament even feel that there may have been a later ceremony at Gilgal that reenacted the crossing of the Jordan. Such a ceremony might have been held in connection with the observance of the Passover in the spring (see 5:10).

The people of Israel made this site their own. It came to have major significance for them. For instance, it was the base of operations for later military expeditions (10:6-9; 14:6). Samuel served as judge at Gilgal (1 Sam. 7:16). It was one of the cities on his regular circuit. The private ceremony when Samuel first anointed Saul king took place there (10:8). So did Saul's official selection involving all the people (11:14-15). Gilgal was also Saul's first transgression (13:8-9). During the eighth century Gilgal was immensely popular as the goal of religious pilgrimages (Amos 4:4-5; 5:4-5; Hosea 4:15; 12:11).

In verse 2C we come back to the twelve stones taken out of the streambed. Joshua set them up there at Gilgal. He repeated his instructions about using the natural curiosity of the children as an opportunity to teach them spiritual truth. He emphasized the results of God's activity on his own people. This time he drew the obvious and close parallel between what had happened to them at the Jordan and what had happened earlier at the Sea. In both cases the Lord dried up the waters and Israel passed over on dry ground (vv. 22-23). The individual people were different, and so were their needs and circumstances, but the Lord and his power were just the same. He is worthy of all fear and reverence from those who are his own (v. 24).

The last verse of chapter 4 and the first verse of chapter 5 emphasize the results of God's activity on the enemy peoples. Joshua assured Israel that all the peoples of the earth would know that the Lord's hand is mighty. Verse 1 of chapter 5 applies this recognition specifically to the city rulers of the Amorites and the Canaanites. Note that the verse locates the Amorites to the west, in the hill country, and the Canaanites in the coastal plains.

When these petty kings heard about the miraculous crossing of the river, panic seized them. Their courage completely failed them because of what God was doing for Israel. This doesn't mean they didn't resist the Israelite invasion. They resisted it fiercely, but they were never able to fight against Israel with confidence and zeal.

As our story progresses, all of the elements continue to fall into their proper place. The stage is steadily being set for the actual taking of the land.

Spiritual Preparation (5:2-15)

Chapter 6 begins the story of the actual taking of the land of Canaan. Chapter 5 concludes the lengthy account of the preparations for that invasion. Significantly, it deals with three important spiritual experiences. The first two are instances of the people being obedient to the long-neglected law. The third is a remarkable encounter and act of worship on the part of the people's leader, Joshua. These three accounts stress again two of the major emphases of this book: If Israel is to succeed in her task, she must be obedient to God's law. If she is obedient, she may be certain of his presence and leadership.

Circumcision of the new generation (5:2-9).—God's command to Joshua in 5:2 was to prepare for the circumcision of the men of the nation. Circumcision was the minor surgery performed on Jewish males, usually a week after birth. It had been neglected for a generation. In this, as in other ways, there was a lot of catching up to do.

Circumcision is an ancient practice and was widespread in the world of the Near East. It was observed by the Egyptians and by most of the Semitic peoples. There are pictorial records of Egyptian observance all the way back to the third millennium BC.

For Israel, circumcision was an act of initiation into the covenant community. In the context of the conquest of Canaan, Israel had to have this mark of membership in the covenant community if she were to expect God's help. Circumcision was also preparation for the observance of the Passover (vv. 10-12), since no uncircumcised male could partake of that meal (Ex. 12:43-49).

For the Israelites, circumcision had been instituted by Abraham (Gen. 17:9-14; 21:4). It had been practiced by Moses (Ex. 4:25-26) and by all the people he led during the Exodus (v. 5). But if this is true, why did Joshua have to begin all over again with the practice ("the second time," v. 2)? Because the rite had not been observed during the years of wandering.

The people of the Exodus had become rebellious and neglectful. They did not listen to the voice of the Lord. They had not properly instructed their offspring in the ways of God. As a result, they had been punished by not being allowed to see the Promised Land. They had died in the desert. A new generation had arisen to take their place. But the members of the new generation, too, had to be consecrated before they could continue to find their proper place in the purposes of God (vv. 4-7).

Notice in verses 2-3 that Joshua used flint knives to perform the surgery, although such implements were no longer in general use. Bronze tools had been available for 2,000 years, and iron tools came into general use within another hundred years, but many religious practices retained the older materials and older approaches of familiar custom and tradition (see Ex. 4:25). The name Gibeath-haaraloth (v. 3) means "the hill of the foreskins." It was an area near Gilgal where the circumcision ceremony took place.

We also need to note the description of Canaan which the record gives in passing in 5:6. It was "a land flowing with milk and honey." It received abundant rainfall, in comparison with the desert where the people had wandered for so long. It was fertile and productive. There was abundant grass for the cattle which produced the milk. There were fruits and flowers to make possible the honey. There were grain, grape, and olive crops, the staples of the farmer of that area then and now. Yes, it was a fruitful land, as the people were just beginning to realize.

After the ceremony of mass circumcision, the people rested for three days so the healing process could be completed. Verse 9 is the Lord's final comment on the circumcision ceremony. On that day, he said, he had rolled away the reproach of Egypt from them.

This expression has perplexed Bible commentators. Some feel it refers to the condition of slavery when their Egyptian masters would not let them participate in their religious practices. But the circumcision associated with the Exodus should have removed any such reproach. Other interpreters see this reproach as related to the uncleanness of a foreign country, the taunts of the Egyptians, or the inferior nature of Egyptian circumcision.

The best explanation seems to be this: The reproach was the status of the enslaved and wandering people who had not yet become an official part of the covenant community. They had remained uncircumcised through many years. This was remedied by the significant experience at Gilgal.

Notice that in verse 9 we have another explanation for the name of the Israelite camp, Gilgal. The name does come from the Hebrew verb meaning "to roll," even though our previous definition of "circle" is a preferable translation. However, the people associated the name of their encampment with the Lord's assertion that he had rolled away from them the reproach of

Egypt. Now they had assumed their place as a full and free people.

Observance of the Passover (5:10-12).—When the circumcision of the males was completed, the people were ready for a second significant religious observance, the keeping of the Passover. This, too, was a ceremony of long-standing. And its observance, too, constituted faithful obedience to God's commands following long years of neglect.

On the fourteenth day of the month of Abib (later Nisan), at evening, there on the plains of Jericho, the deliverance from the tenth plague was properly commemorated. The coming of the death angel, the blood on the door facings and lintels, the horror and tragedy in the Egyptian homes, the rejoicing and relief among the Israelites, and finally the release from the generations of grinding slavery—all of this was remembered and celebrated as God had instructed Moses.

Some people see in verse 11 the observance of the Feast of Unleavened Bread, which is traditionally associated with the Feast of the Passover. One looks forward to the deliverance from Egypt and the other to the actual entry into the Promised Land. Jews generally observed the two holidays over a single eight-day period. Both of these festivals have close associations with the spring harvest and gratitude to God for his bounty. We do not know whether this verse refers to an official observance of the Feast of Unleavened Bread, but we do know that on the fifteenth day of the month the Israelites ate the produce of the land. They were making the significant transition from nomadic desert wanderings to a more settled agricultural life. The land of milk and honey was becoming a practical reality to them. They ate a meal of unleavened cakes and parched grain.

It was truly the end of an epoch. The first observance of the Passover in the new land marked the closing of an old era and the dawning of an entirely new one. The fact that on the day after the Passover the manna ceased further underlines the significance of the transition from one period to another. Manna had been their mainstay for a generation, but it was to be no more (Ex. 16:35). From then on they would eat the bounty of the land around them.

The appearance of the commander of the Lord's army (5:13-15).—The third significant spiritual event of this chapter involved only Joshua. He was out doing some personal reconnoitering of the city of Jericho. He was assessing the task just before them and thinking through his strategy for the first phase of the actual taking of the land.

During this excursion Joshua saw a man confronting him, his sword in his hand. Joshua mistook him for a human soldier and immediately put to this stranger a form of the traditional challenge, "Friend or foe?" (see v. 13).

Joshua must have been surprised by the reply. The man said he was the commander of the army of the Lord. In that role he had come to Joshua, not in the role of an ally or a foe. The man's reply moved his relationship with Joshua and the people into an entirely different dimension.

Joshua responded in the only proper way. He fell down before this commander-in-chief (literally, "prince"). He fell on his face to the earth and worshiped. Notice also that Joshua asked for instructions. He asked what his orders were. God was dramatically symbolizing his presence and guidance, and Joshua was placing himself at the Lord's disposal.

The strange figure commanded Joshua to take his shoes off. The place where he had been standing had been made holy by the presence of the Lord. Of course Joshua complied. This command immediately makes us think of Moses' experience with God at the burning bush (Ex. 3:1-6). In fact, almost every element of the two stories is parallel, except that Joshua received no commission (although some people see the commission in Josh. 6:2-5).

Joshua's encounter is what we call a theophany. It means an appearance of God or a self-revelation of God, showing that God is present in an audible and/or visible way.

We would tend to describe the "man" Joshua saw as an angel, a heavenly messenger sent from God. However, the Hebrews did not make as much of a distinction as we do between the appearance of God and the appearance of one of his messengers. Abraham's visitors are described variously as men, angels, and the Lord (see Gen. 18:1-33 and Heb. 13:2). We see the same thing in Gideon's strange worship experience (Judg. 6:11-18).

The meaning of Joshua's encounter is much more clear. "The army of the Lord" (v. 14) is a reference to the hosts of angelic beings ready to fight for God's people (see Gen. 32:1-2). At times the stars are spoken of as heavenly hosts, summoned to do God's bidding (Isa. 40:26). But here we have the idea of invisible angels who fight for God's people (2 Kings 6:17). The expression may also include the troops of Israel. In other words, God and his heavenly hosts stood ready to fight *with* and *for* Israel's armies.

The next entry in Joshua's appointment book was the attack on Jericho. Surely, after the rite of circumcision, the observance of the Passover, and his encounter with the commander of the hosts of the Lord, Joshua was ready for it. The spiritual preparation had been made. The prelude to the conquest was complete.

The Three-Pronged Conquest (6:1 to 12:24)

The first five chapters of Joshua only set the stage for the most important section of the book, the actual conquest of the land. This conquest was accomplished through the notable strategy of cutting the land in two at the middle and then subduing the southern and northern sections in turn.

Central (6:1 to 9:27)

We have already noted that Jericho was the guardian fortress between the lower Jordan Valley and the central hill country of Canaan. You can tell how important the location was by how old the city was. Jericho is one of the oldest inhabited sites in the world. It formed a major roadblock to any Israelite success. It had to be dealt with before any further steps forward could be made. With Jericho in Israelite hands, the central highlands would be much more vulnerable.

The fall of Jericho (6:1-27).—The battle of Jericho is one of the best known battles in all of history. All of us have heard its songs sung and its story told. Not only were the circumstances of the battle dramatic and the results important, the battle was also of tremendous psychological significance. It was Israel's first engagement after crossing the Jordan, it was a resounding victory, and it was accomplished strictly through the working of the Lord.

Some people have taken verse 1 to indicate that Joshua had blockaded the city as the first step in his seige. It is more likely that the inhabitants themselves shut the city up completely and allowed no entrance or exit. Perhaps they were too frightened to follow any other course, or perhaps they did not know what else to do. At any rate, their precautions were futile.

In verses 2-7 we have the strategy for the coming "battle" described in detail. These are the advance instructions as to how the people were to proceed and what the outcome would be. The Lord told Joshua that he had already given Jericho, its petty ruler, and all his armed men into his hand.

The people were to make use of a considerable amount of what we would call psychological warfare. Also, their actions had considerable significance as religious ceremony. They were to march around the city and to return to camp without a single belligerent act. They were to do this once a day for six days. On the seventh and climactic day they were to march around seven times.

The priests led this incredible procession. Seven priests were to blow seven trumpets made of curved rams' horns. This is the *shophar* used to give battle signals, mark state occasions, and celebrate religious festivals. It is completely different from the metal musical instruments we call trumpets today.

At the end of the seventh circuit of the city on the seventh day, the priests were to sound a long blast on their trumpets. At that signal, the people were to shout. They were to give the battle cry, a shout with religious overtones that would inspire Israel and further demoralize the defenders. Then the wall of the city would fall down flat. After that, the result of the battle would be a foregone conclusion. Each soldier was to move straight ahead of him toward the center of the city. They would all meet in the middle in a victorious celebration of what the Lord had so clearly done.

After the Lord revealed his plan, Joshua proceeded without question to implement it. He instructed the priests carrying the ark of the covenant which, as always, symbolized the presence of the Lord. He instructed the priests with the rams' horn trumpets, and he commanded the people to go forth to the march.

We cannot leave this part of the chapter without a reference to the repeated use of the number seven. Its use adds a further religious tone to the entire record.

Verses 8-14 describe the carrying out of the strategy outlined previously. This is the actual psychological warfare that preceded the fall of the city and made complete triumph possible. Verses 7 and 9 say that the procession around the city was headed by a vanguard of armed men. Next came the seven priests sounding their *shophars*. Then followed the ark of the covenant, as always carried by four priests. Lastly, there was a rear guard, presumably also armed, and, finally, all the people.

The people were instructed to maintain complete silence during all of this activity. They were not to shout or to speak until the proper time on the seventh day. It had to be spooky. Imagine how the citizens of Jericho felt. Their nerves were shot. I have often wondered what the reaction would be if one athletic team, band, cheering section, and body of fans used this "silent treatment" on their opponents.

Jericho was some six to nine acres in area. It was not large by our modern standards, with a few thousand inhabitants. You could walk entirely around it in fifteen to thirty minutes if you wanted to stay well away from the walls, out of arrow range. Each march around Jericho brought half an hour of unbearably tense silence for the Canaanites, and then the rest of the day and night of sleeplessness and foreboding.

Finally, as verse 15 tells us, the seventh day came. The people got up at dawn and began the climactic series of marches. They knew, and the people inside the city knew, that something dramatic was about to happen. Following the seventh circuit, the signal to shout was given. Verse 10 says it was a command from Joshua. Verses 5 and 20 say it was the blowing of the trumpet. Joshua said, "Shout; for the Lord has given you the city" (v. 16). Verse 20 says the people shouted and all the trumpets were blown.

As soon as these sounds were heard, the city wall fell down flat. The people swarmed over the rubble, with hardly any resistance. In this way they took the city.

The Jordan Valley is a rift valley. It was formed by the collapse of a section of the earth's surface between parallel fault lines in the rock structure beneath it. It is geologically unstable and therefore an earthquake zone. Numerous earthquakes have been recorded in the area. Some Bible students feel that an earthquake may have been the instrument the Lord used to accomplish the collapse of the city wall. If so, the timing was miraculous. Others feel that the Lord flattened the wall without natural means. Either way God gave Israel the city, as he had promised.

Verses 17-19 form a parenthesis in the fast-moving story that relates to a matter we hinted at before, the concept of holy war. It is a central idea in the book of Joshua. Verse 17 says that the city and all that was in it were put under the ban. They were devoted to the Lord for destruction.

The idea of holy war was common in earlier times, but is completely foreign to us. In fact, it is not too much to say that in ancient times all war was linked with religion. Every campaign was fought on behalf of God. It was instituted at the command of God and begun with a sacrifice (1 Sam. 7:7-10; 13:8-9). Of course, during these battles the Lord fought for Israel. He gave Israel the victory.

One feature of the holy war was that the participants had to be in a state of holiness, of ceremonial purity. It is more than a little foreign to our modern thinking that soldiers be consecrated as ministers of the Lord. Even the camp had to be clean (Deut. 23:9-14). We can see how, with such a background, Israel, as the people of God, came to see their wars as the wars of God. The enemies of Israel were considered the enemies of God.

The conclusion of such a holy war was not wild rejoicing in victory or the dividing up of the spoils of battle. Rather, it was the observance of the ban. The ban or curse separated a thing. It made it taboo. It removed it from normal use and reserved it exclusively for use by God. In Arabic, the sacred areas of Jerusalem and Mecca are designated by a related word. The biblical term is especially associated with warfare. The Hebrews evidently felt that placing an enemy city under the ban might make victory more likely.

Other peoples also practiced the ban. At a later time the king of Moab dedicated the Israelite city of Nebo to his god Chemosh. This dedicatory rite could involve not only inanimate objects but also living beings (Num. 21:2-3; Deut. 7:1-5). It could include not only the enemy soldier but his women and children and his cattle (v. 21).

As is the case with so many other laws God had given, Israel was not consistent in applying this principle (Num. 31:7-12,17-18; Deut. 21:10-14; 1 Sam. 15:8-9). The practice was abandoned early in the period of the monarchy.

The ban was instituted at Jericho. Joshua said that the city and everything in it was devoted to the Lord for destruction. Rahab and the members of her family were to be the only survivors (v. 17). Articles of valuable metal were to be placed in the Lord's treasury (vv. 19,24). The people were to keep themselves from the booty of Jericho. If taken it would be a source of temptation, sin, and destruction for Israel (Deut. 13:17). We will soon see how this curse worked itself out in the case of Achan.

The practice of the ban obviously constituted a strong discipline for the soldiers. It was an irrevocable renunciation of what was thought to be an almost inherent right to spoils. It did away with the lust for conquest for materialistic gain. It also removed a considerable source of temptation to idolatry (Deut. 20:16-18).

The account of the destruction of the inhabitants of Jericho brings us back to the moral question we referred to in the Introduction. It seems barbaric to us today to destroy whole populations, especially in the name of the Lord. There is no completely satisfactory answer to our difficulty. However, we remember: the commonness of this practice in that part of the world at that time; the constant temptation to idolatry, and the fact that faith in God had to be kept pure at all costs, with no measures considered too drastic in order to ensure that purity; the element of God's judgment on the Canaanites because of their wickedness (Gen. 15:16; Lev. 18:24-25; Deut. 9:5); and the fact that Joshua lived long before Jesus who taught us to love our enemies.

We remember also that Israel believed that God was the Lord of history. He was actively engaged in the affairs of his people and of all people. We continue to marvel that God is able to use sinful human agents and means to accomplish his purpose. This is not an ideal world, but God is actively involved in working out his purpose. A part of that purpose was to choose Israel to be his special people and promise them a land. The fulfillment of that promise involved expelling the Canaanites.

There is absolutely no justification for the adoption of this ancient concept of "holy war" by any modern nation.

The final paragraph of this chapter deals with Rahab and her family. Joshua sent the two spies to Rahab's house. Evidently the wall that adjoined it had not collapsed. They were to bring out her and hers, according to their previous agreement. You will note in verse 23 that this group stayed for a while outside the camp. They were virtual proselytes, but they were still foreigners. Foreigners were unclean and were forbidden to enter the camp until the proper purification ceremonies had been completed (Num. 31:19; Deut. 23:10-11). Following this initiation, Rahab and her party became a part of Israel, and her descendants were well-known at the time of the writing of this book (Josh. 6:25).

The chapter concludes with Joshua's curse on anyone who tried to rebuild Jericho. He would suffer the loss of both his oldest and youngest sons (see 1 Kings 16:34). Archaeological records do show that Jericho lay in ruins until the ninth century. Biblical references to Jericho's resettlement evidently refer to a reoccupation of the general area, not the specific site (Josh. 18:21; 2 Sam. 10:5).

Defeat and victory at Ai (7:1 to 8:29).—With Jericho in ruins, the people were ready to move "from conquest unto victory," as an eloquent East Texas preacher used to put it. But a funny thing happened to them on the way to the next winner's circle: They were soundly defeated. It happened in the first battle of Ai.

Lest we be too surprised at the turn of events, 7:1 lets us in on a secret. The Lord's anger burned against the people of Israel. They had violated the ban on Jericho. They had treacherously taken some of the spoils devoted to the Lord. Everyone had not participated in this flagrant sin. In fact, only Achan had. Thanks to him, Israel was defeated.

This story illustrates again one of the key themes of the Deuteronomic outlook: God's conditional blessings. God will help Israel if . . . *if* . . . IF she is obedient. Her success in capturing and continuing in the land depended on absolute loyalty. The slightest deviation would bring disaster for the guilty individual and for all the people.

Ai, up in the edge of the highlands, was Joshua's next target. He sent spies to look it over. However, the spies returned with an overly optimistic report. They said that since Ai was such a small place, and since the sixteen mile climb from eight hundred feet below sea level at Jericho to 2,500 feet above sea level at Ai was so rugged, all the army needn't go. Only a small force would be required.

It was a classic case of overconfidence and self-reliance. Joshua was trying to win today's game on yesterday's score. He apparently prepared no strategy for the battle.

Joshua sent only 3,000 men in a frontal assault on little Ai. All 3,000 retreated in disarray before a fierce counterattack. They scampered from the city gate back down the steep slope, pursued as far as some unknown stone quarries called Shebarim, and thirty-six of the men were killed.

Thirty-six casualties do not sound like many, not even out of a force of 3,000. However, though the military significance of the defeat was small, the psychological significance was immense. The defeat brought consternation to Israel. It was their turn to be afraid. Verse 5 says that "the hearts of the people melted, and became as water." And this verse is not talking about the Canaanites; it is talking about the people of the Lord.

Joshua and the other leaders fell to their knees in prayer. They showed the traditional signs of mourning: torn clothes, dust on the head, and falling on the face (1 Sam. 4:12; 2 Sam. 1:2). We do not have many examples of Joshua's prayers, but they were intense. Here he sounded a bit like the people who followed Moses in the desert. He didn't understand what had happened. He even seems to have been afraid that the Lord had forsaken them.

Joshua asked the Lord why he had brought the people over the Jordan if he were going to give them into the hands of their enemies. Why God's graciousness, and why the miracles, if they were to be so easily destroyed? It would have been better for them just to stay on the other side of the Jordan (v. 7) than to be humiliated before the enemy.

Joshua was afraid that the Canaanites, at such a morale disadvantage up to this point, would experience a new surge of courage, unite, and drive Israel out (7:9). They would completely annihilate Israel—they would cut their name off from the earth. What is more, the Lord's name would be cut off, too. A god who allowed his people to be defeated was thought to be weak.

The Lord responded to Joshua's prayer with a call for action. There was sin in the camp. Nothing could be done until it was taken care of. Israel had transgressed the Lord's covenant. The term "covenant" here evidently refers to the command of placing Jericho under the ban (6:17-19). They had stolen some of the devoted things and had lied about it in the process. They had made what belonged to the Lord their own (7:11).

This was the explanation for the defeat at Ai. By taking the forbidden item, Achan had come to share its curse and in turn had infected all Israel with it as well. The Lord's presence with his people was not automatic. In fact, he would be with them no longer unless they destroyed the forbidden articles (7:17).

The Lord ordered Joshua to get up, ceremonially prepare the people, and get them ready for the exposure and destruction of the evildoer. The designation of the one responsible was to be followed by his being burned with fire, "he and all that he has, because he has transgressed the covenant of the Lord, and because he has done a shameful thing in Israel" (7:15). His sin was so flagrant and damaging that there was no other alternative.

The next morning Joshua began the process of selection. It involved some sort of lot, perhaps the Urim and Thummim (1 Sam. 28:6). Marked objects were cast on the ground or drawn from a container. This was the technique God used to select the tribe of Judah from among the twelve tribes, the clan of the Zerahites from among the clans of Judah, and the household of Zabdi from among the Zerahites. And finally Achan was selected as the guilty person.

Joshua urged Achan to give praise to God by making a full confession. He should glorify God because God is all-knowing and had brought the secret to light. What is more, his judgment is just, as Achan was urged to concur. Joshua called him "my son" (7:19), and in response to this fair and tender treatment Achan made a full confession. He described the beautiful mantle from Shinar (later called Babylon), the bar of silver weighing some five pounds, and the bar of gold weighing a pound and a quarter. (Shekel here is a unit of weight, not a coin.)

Notice that Achan's first sin had been to break the Tenth Commandment (7:21). His covetousness had led him to take the objects for himself, even though he knew that such an act was specifically forbidden. He had hidden them in a hole under his tent.

Joshua sent messengers to confirm Achan's story. When they brought the forbidden articles, Joshua and all the people "laid them down before the Lord" (7:23). Those items had been devoted to the Lord before the destruction of Jericho, they still belonged to the Lord, and here they were symbolically restored to him.

Then came judgment time for Achan. He was treated in the same way as the forbidden objects he had contaminated himself with (Deut. 3:15-16).

He and his family, his animals, his tent, and all his possessions were taken to the valley of Achor some five miles to the south of Jericho. Joshua's pronouncement of sentence on Achan is seen in 7:25. It is also a play on his name and the name of the valley where he died—both terms are related to the Hebrew word for trouble. The place of execution is aptly named. What he did meant trouble for Achan, trouble for his innocent family, and trouble for all of Israel.

All the congregation participated in the stoning and burning. When the execution was carried out, the people placed a heap of stones over his remains, which was visible at the valley of Achor until the lifetime of the author of Joshua. Then the Lord turned his burning anger away from Israel (7:26).

Before we leave this remarkable story, we need to say a word about how Achan's sin affected all of Israel and how all his family members were involved in his punishment. Was it right for them to die because he had violated the ban? In this case the punishment seems far worse than the crime.

We do know that one person's sin always has consequences in the lives of those around him. We also know that the Hebrews had a much stronger sense of corporate identity than we do today. We so emphasize individualism that we have trouble understanding the way they looked at family solidarity and the part one person plays in the life of the community and even the nation.

To the Hebrews a person was so bound to his group that he shared all of its sorrows and punishments as well as its joys and blessings. The entire group was responsible for the sin of one of its members. There is some emphasis on individual responsibility in the Old Testament—in fact, there is a better balance here than most people realize (Deut. 24:16)—but by far the stronger emphasis is on the family unit.

When the cause of the defeat at Ai had been removed, the people could resume the task of capturing the city. This time they had the Lord's presence, his favor, his specific direction, and his assurance of victory. The Lord spoke to Joshua to urge him not to be discouraged by the previous setback (8:1-2). He and the people probably weren't overconfident this time. We can see evidences of a new care and humility in the narrative.

"Go up to Ai" (8:1) was a literal necessity, since it was far up in the hills above Gilgal. The Lord's assurance was that the outcome of the second battle would be the same as the outcome of the battle of Jericho. The only difference was that though Ai, too, was placed under the ban, it was a limited ban. The city and its king were to be destroyed, but the spoil and cattle the people could take for themselves (Deut. 2:34-35; 3:6-7).

Joshua had learned to pay much more attention to his strategy—no hurry-up job for him this time. For one thing, he took his entire army with him (8:1,3). He planned an ambush of thirty thousand men according to verse 3, twelve thousand according to verse 12. Again we have that troublesome Hebrew word usually translated "thousand" but also meaning a family, a fighting unit, or a segment of a tribe.

The ambush force was sent ahead, to position itself by night. Those soldiers were to lie in wait to the west of the city, behind it and opposite its main gate. They were to remain hidden but were to be ready (8:4,9).

The rest of the soldiers would serve as a decoy. They would go against the city more directly. When the men of Ai resisted, they would fall back as they had in the first battle. Naturally, the defenders would pursue again, expecting another easy victory. The attackers would thus draw them away from their primary responsibility of defending the city (8:5-6).

When this had taken place, the troops in ambush were to rise up and attack the defenseless city. They were to set the city on fire, a clear signal both to the defenders and the attackers. By means of this clever strategy the Lord would give the city into their hands (8:7-8).

These basic plans were carried out, as we see beginning in 8:10. The main body of the fighting force camped north of Ai, across a ravine from the city. The ruse worked like a charm. The king of Ai attacked, and this time he was the one who was careless and hasty. He intended to once again chase his foes down the slopes toward the Arabah, the depression of which the Jordan valley is a part (8:14).

Joshua's men pretended to be beaten. They fell back toward the desert areas to the east of the highlands. All the men defending the city rushed after them. Verse 17 says that "there was not a man left in Ai or Bethel, who did not go out after Israel; they left the city open."

Joshua had evidently stationed himself so that he could be seen by both sections of his troops. When the proper time came, the Lord commanded him to signal with his javelin. He pointed it toward the city. This was the sign for the troops in ambush to attack. They entered the unguarded city, and the battle was as good as over. Quickly they set the city on fire (8:18-20).

When the men of Ai looked back from their pursuit, they saw the smoke of the city rising up into the sky. Their hearts fell. They so lost spirit that "they had no power to flee this way or that" (8:20). This may mean that they were so terror-stricken they were unable to even attempt escape. Or it may mean that the Israelites so boxed them in that no escape was possible. The Israelites turned back from their supposed retreat and began an attack of their own.

The men of Ai were caught between the main body of soldiers they had been pursuing and the smaller group from the ambush that came out of the burning city to attack them from behind. It is not surprising that none of them survived or escaped. Only the king was taken alive (8:22-23).

The word "slaughter" is used to describe the second battle of Ai, an appropriate choice of terms (8:24). All the inhabitants of the city fell to the edge of the sword, those fighting out in the open and those who had remained in the city. Twelve thousand men and women in all were killed.

When Joshua pointed with his javelin as a signal for the group in ambush to attack, he did not draw it back until the battle was completely won (8:26). This is another obvious parallel with the experience of Moses, who held up his rod until "General" Joshua completely defeated the Amalekites (Ex. 17:11-13).

The cattle and spoil of the city were appropriated by the people. The city itself was burned to the ground. Joshua made the city a heap of ruins (8:28), as it remained until the time this book was written. In fact, that is what the name Ai means, "the ruin."

As for the king of Ai, he was executed and his body hanged on a tree until sundown. This was standard operating procedure in those times. It served to demoralize the conquered people and terminate the old regime. It was an act of extreme humiliation and even indicated that the curse of God was on the victim. Then, when evening came, his body was taken down (Deut. 21:22-23) and buried under a heap of stones near the gate of the city. The battle had been violent and bloody, and the victory was complete.

The covenant renewed at Shechem (8:30-35).—To our shock, this paragraph appears right in the middle of the progression of conquest stories. It tells about an obvious covenant renewal ceremony at Shechem, twenty miles north of Ai. Our surprise is due to the fact that we have heard nothing so far about any conquest of this area. Yet the people seem to have moved quite easily northward, with none of the resistance they had been facing.

This brief section reminds us of the much longer account of covenant renewal we find in 24:1-28. The point of this first record is evidently to let us know that very early, as soon as they had gained a secure foothold in the hill country, the people participated in a covenant ceremony just as Moses had commanded (Deut. 11:29; 27:1-8).

Shechem was an ancient site located between Mount Ebal on the north and Mount Gerizim on the south. There on Mount Ebal Joshua erected an altar, as Moses had commanded. It was an altar of whole, that is, uncut stones. The idea was that the stones would somehow be defiled if metal tools were applied to them (Ex. 20:25). Burnt offerings and peace offerings were made to the Lord from this new and special altar (vv. 30-31).

With the people looking on, Joshua wrote a copy of the law of Moses upon stones. Most people feel these were standing stones, like the ones set up previously at Gilgal, not the actual stones of the altar. These stones were probably treated with plaster, as in Deuteronomy 27:3.

What did Joshua write? Probably not the entire Pentateuch or book of Deuteronomy. It is more likely that he wrote a copy of the Ten Commandments and perhaps also the sections of Deuteronomy that deal with the blessings and the curses, the consequences of obedience and disobedience (Deut. 27:11-26; 28:3-6,15-19).

Verse 33 makes a vital point. The covenant was not limited to native-born Israelites. There was provision also for naturalized Israelites. The sojourner was the person of foreign birth who had cast his lot with Israel. Most scholars feel that this is the explanation for the fact that the people were able to move from Ai to Shechem without opposition. The people who settled this area in the fourteenth century BC were distantly related to the Israelites. What is more, there is no record in Joshua or Judges of any battles of conquest around Shechem. These people, who had had no part in the Exodus, evidently joined with those who had in recognizing the Lord and entering into covenant with him. When they did, they received full covenant privileges. Everyone—women, children, foreigners—was involved (v. 35).

The ark of the covenant was located in the midst of the people, between the twin mountains. Half of the people gathered on one slope, half on the other, as Moses had desired. Then Joshua read all the words of the law without leaving anything out. He seems to have emphasized particularly the blessings of obedience and the curses of disobedience we have encountered so often in this book with its Deuteronomic outlook (vv. 33-35).

God had clearly indicated at Jericho and Ai that he would do his part. He would be faithful to his promises. At Shechem the people pledged themselves anew to be just as loyal.

The treaty with the Gibeonites (9:1-27).—This is one of the most interesting stories in this book, a story of desperation, deceit, naivete, and yet loyalty to one's word. The outcome of the story gives us some important insights into the makeup of God's covenant people.

The chapter begins with a note on the effect of the second battle of Ai on the Canaanites generally. Their city kings finally became frightened enough over Israel's easy successes to shake off their despair and begin to unite. Their proposed unity never seems to have materialized, but we will learn of their resistance to Joshua in chapters 10 and 11. "Beyond the Jordan" (v. 1) in this case refers to the western side of the river.

Verse 1 says that Canaanite forces from the entire land were beginning to form against Israel. The three geographical areas mentioned take in all of western Palestine. The hill country refers to the central highlands. The lowlands, usually called the Shephelah, were the foothills between the central highlands and the Philistine plain. The coastal plain stretched along the sea up to Lebanon. Once again some of the various groupings of native peoples are listed.

But one league of towns led by the important city of Gibeon reacted in a different way. Those people, too, knew what had happened at Jericho and Ai. However, they had no hope of defeating Israel. They decided, instead, to use trickery to secure a peace treaty with the invaders, even if it meant resigning themselves to a subordinate social status.

Gibeon was in the hill country some six miles north of Jerusalem and six and one-half miles southwest of Ai. The other three cities were in a five-mile radius of Gibeon. They are named in v. 17. Chephirah was four and one-half miles west southwest of Gibeon. Beeroth was probably the same distance northeast. Kiriath-jearim is seven miles west of Jerusalem and five miles southwest of Gibeon.

You will note that in v. 7 the Gibeonite representatives are called Hivites. This is probably the group more commonly called Horites in the Old Testament and Hurrians in extrabiblical sources. They are referred to as Amorites in some places (2 Sam. 21:2) but were evidently not of Canaanite stock.

Gibeonite representatives got together food that was dry and moldy. They collected goatskin containers, sandals, and clothes that had been worn-out, torn, and patched. They wanted to give every appearance of having made a lengthy, difficult journey. They later claimed that they had taken the dry, moldy bread fresh from the oven, and that their wineskins, sandals, and clothes had been brand-new when they began their trek.

They approached Joshua in camp at Gilgal. They claimed to have come from a far country, and asked Israel to make a peace treaty with them. The people of Israel were immediately suspicious. What if these strangers lived nearby? Then Israel couldn't make a covenant with them. Distant non-

Canaanite cities could secure peace with Israel if they agreed to be subordinate (Deut. 20:10-15), but the resident nations of Canaan had to be utterly destroyed (Deut. 7:1-2; 20:16-18).

The Gibeonites were not only good actors, they were true diplomats. "We are your servants," they assured Joshua (v. 8). That may have been a customary courtesy, or it may have indicated a concession on their part in order to conclude the peace treaty. Verses 9 and 10 remind us of Rahab's confession in 2:10. They said they had heard of the Lord and of what he had done in Egypt and Transjordan. They very wisely left out any reference to what had happened since Israel crossed the river—no distant foreigner would be expected to have heard news like that.

The representatives of the Gibeonite league said that when word of the Lord and his mighty acts reached them, their elders and people urged them to go to meet Israel and seek an alliance. The skeptical men of Israel tasted the stale bread and were convinced. One thing they did not do, however, was consult the Lord (v. 14).

The Gibeonite mission was successful. Joshua concluded the peace treaty with them. He made with them the covenant they requested. They would not rest under the ban that applied to the entire land of Canaan. The leaders of the congregation of Israel all gave their word that they would be permitted to live.

It was only a short time later that the Israelites learned that they had been tricked. They learned that, rather than being from a far country, the Gibeonites were close neighbors. They lived just a few short miles away. Some Israelite representatives hurried to the cities to see for themselves (vv. 16-17).

The people of Israel were incensed and even murmured against their leaders who had hastily agreed to the treaty. However, the leaders judged that since they had sworn by the Lord, they should honor the agreement. The Gibeonite group would not be killed. They knew that if they violated their oath, they would be under the wrath of God because of it. Saul had to suffer that wrath specifically because he violated this agreement (2 Sam. 21:1).

As a compromise, Joshua and the other leaders ordered that the people of the Gibeonite league assume a servant role. The Israelite oath spared them from death but not from penalty. They would be reduced to the lowest rung of the social ladder. "Hewers of wood and drawers of water" (vv. 21,23,27) is probably a cliché for servanthood. It refers to what was considered to be women's work in those days and carried with it considerable social stigma. The phrases may also mean that they were to disband their army and rely on Israel for defense.

Verses 23 and 27 make a point of associating this Gibeonite service with the sanctuary of the Lord. These are probably references initially to a sanctuary at Gibeon and later to the Temple Solomon built. You will remember that Solomon went to Gibeon to offer sacrifices and pray for wisdom (1 Kings 3:4-14). Joshua's statement that they would always be slaves probably indicates that they were to furnish temple workers in perpetuity.

So this chapter of the conquest story explains the activity of Gibeonites in sanctuary service. It also explains their presence as a part of the community of Israel. Though they had not shared in the Exodus, they did share in the covenant. They are mentioned some forty-five times in eight different Old Testament books. We know they were considered to be a full part of the covenant community because they are named among those who returned to Judah from exile in Babylon as late as the days of Nehemiah (Neh. 3:7; 7:25). Once again we see the inclusive nature of Israelite society and Israelite faith.

We have all heard this passage used to defend racial segregation or prejudice. The Gibeonite status as servants was the result not of their ethnic background but of their deception. Furthermore, they came to be accepted as full members of the covenant community. To apply Joshua 9 to race relations in any negative and discriminatory sense is a travesty of Bible interpretation.

Southern (10:1-43)

The destruction of Jericho had opened the interior of Canaan to the Israelites. The capture of Ai had secured for them a foothold in the central hill country. The treaty with the Gibeonite league had expanded their control to a major east-west corridor across Canaan and threatened to cut the country completely in two.

Joshua's intention was to turn southward and deal with the resistance in that section. Before he had a chance to do so, however, that resistance united and moved against him. The battle was quickly joined, and the campaign for southern Canaan was well under way.

The defeat of the five kings (10:1-27).—Adoni-zedek, the king of Jerusalem, had kept up with all the war news. He knew what had happened to Jericho and Ai, their rulers, and their inhabitants. He was especially incensed by the action of the Gibeonite league. Those four cities had collaborated with the enemy. This meant that a large and strategically located city was under Israelite control, together with a respected military force (v. 2). Both Gibeon and Kiriath-jearim were located at the heads of valleys that gave access through the foothills to the central highlands.

Adoni-zedek was the moving force behind a new coalition of Canaanite city kings, the first such coalition to be successfully carried through and to take the offensive against the invaders. Actually, their attack was on Gibeon, not Israel directly. They wanted to punish Gibeon for their peace treaty with Israel (10:5), and of course they wanted to retake the city.

Jerusalem was the most prominent city of southern Canaan. This is its first mention in the Old Testament. Hebron was on the same central mountain ridge some twenty miles to the south. The other three allied cities were west of Jerusalem in the foothills. Jarmuth was sixteen miles from Jerusalem, Lachish twenty-seven miles, and Eglon seven miles west southwest of Lachish.

Because Israel had accepted the cities of the Gibeonite league as vassals, an attack on them was the same as an attack on Israel. When the seige started, Gibeon appealed to Joshua as she had every right to do (v. 6). However, Joshua was probably delighted with the chance to attack five such important Amorite kings, especially since he had the Lord's assurance of complete victory (v. 8).

Joshua was at his best as a military leader during this southern campaign. By means of a forced march over twenty miles of mountainous terrain, he reached Gibeon before daybreak. True to his word, the Lord fought for Israel. He threw the enemy into panic. They were routed before the unexpected Israelite advance.

The pass of Beth-horon is five miles northwest of Gibeon. It leads down through the valley of Aijalon to the coastal plain. The pursuit of the enemy moved through that pass, westward down the valley of Aijalon toward the coast and then southward as far as Azekah and Makkedah. During the steep descent, huge hailstones pounded the fleeing Amorites. In fact, more were killed by the hailstones than by the Israelite swords (v. 11). Again we have a clear indication that the Lord was the source of Israel's victories.

Verses 12-14 appear at the end of the description of the battle like the poetic song of Moses after the deliverance at the sea (Ex. 15:1-18), but some interpreters think they refer to an incident at the beginning of the contest. Four lines are quoted from the ancient book of Jasher, a poetry anthology of stories about the heroes of Israel. It was probably compiled during the reigns of David or Solomon. It is known only because of this reference and another in 2 Samuel 1:18-27. Joshua commanded the sun to hold its position in the east, over Gibeon, and the moon its position in the west, over the valley of Aijalon. Thus Israel was better able to complete the victory over her foes.

Needless to say, the "long day of Joshua" had been a subject of much discussion. The record presents a problem to many people in a day when we know the earth, not the sun, moves in orbit. There are three major theories that try to explain the difficulty.

One theory holds that the earth and moon actually stood still in their orbits around the sun. A literal reading of verse 13 would make this freezing of planetary orbits extend to a full twenty-four hour period. Religious authorities in Galileo's day used these verses to prove him wrong when he claimed that the sun does not revolve around the earth.

A second theory points out that the source for this quotation is a book of Hebrew poems ("Book of Jashar"). Poetic language is often figurative and not to be taken literally. An example is Judges 5:20, which says that the stars fought against Sisera. This view says that Joshua prayed for help and the Lord helped him accomplish a great deal in a short time. Even today, we still use the expression "This has been the longest day,"—although all our days are of equal length.

A third theory relates not to daylight being lengthened but to the sun being darkened. In this view, Joshua's prayer was not for more daylight but for the delay of daylight. He and his men had marched all night and wanted to be able to attack the enemy under cover of darkness, before the dawn revealed their presence and took away the element of surprise.

This is another place in Scripture where we should not let our difficulty with the interpretation of a passage obscure for us its central meaning. The Lord did help Israel gain a complete victory over her enemies. It is true that Joshua was a shrewd commander and that his men fought fiercely; however, it is even more true that "the Lord fought for Israel" (v. 14).

Verse 15 is also something of a minor problem. It mentions a return all the way to the base camp at Gilgal, before the Amorite rulers were captured and executed. Yet verse 21 locates the camp at Makkedah during the campaign. Perhaps verse 15 is a conclusion for the general battle at Gibeon, while the following verses provide a more detailed wrap-up of the events involved.

The five kings in the coalition hid in a cave at Makkedah. They were quickly located. Joshua had the cave mouth sealed and guarded. This freed the bulk of the troops to further pursue the enemy and prevent all but a few stragglers from reaching the safety of their fortresses. Then, when the "very great slaughter" was finished (v. 20), the army assembled at the new camp at Makkedah. The Lord had truly given their opponents into their hand. Not an inhabitant spoke against the people of Israel (vv. 19,21).

Joshua ordered the cave mouth unsealed and the five kings brought before him. He had his officers and men place their feet on the necks of their captives. This signified complete subjugation. It served to humiliate the victim and further demoralize the foe. Joshua's assurance to his men was that the Lord would do the same to all their enemies (v. 25).

Then the kings were executed and hanged on five trees until sundown, as the king of Ai had been, a further dishonor and a warning to Israel's enemies. Their bodies were buried in the cave. The author of history observed that the cave, its mouth sealed with stones, and the five trees were still well-known in his day.

Conquest of the south Canaanite cities (10:28-39).—The next few verses sketch Joshua's lightning-like campaign to subdue the south. He moved from Makkedah, through the foothills, to take Libnah, Lachish, and Eglon on a line from north to south. They served as frontier fortresses guarding valley approaches from the foothills into the highlands of Judea. Sennacherib of Assyria and Nebuchadnezzar of Babylon later followed the same strategy.

The rulers of the latter two cities had been involved in the short-lived Amorite coalition. All of these cities were placed under the ban and destroyed. The city of Gezer was not taken, as archaeological studies confirm. However, a force from there sent to the aid of Lachish was completely wiped out (v. 33).

Next Joshua turned eastward into the heart of the highlands of Judea to destroy the two chief walled cities there. Hebron was twenty miles south of Jerusalem. It had been a coalition city and had evidently chosen a new king since the execution of its former ruler at Makkedah. Joshua also conquered its dependent villages. Debir, twelve miles southwest of Hebron, was the final target.

This account only highlights Joshua's work. Its parts obviously fall into a consistent literary pattern. We know from later records that other work of conquest was needed at later times (see 15:14-19; Judg. 1:10-20). However, the basic work had been done.

Summary of the southern campaign (10:40-43).—The final paragraph of chapter 10 is a summary conclusion of the campaign which had already been described in detail throughout the chapter. The whole southern area had been taken. This included the central highlands, the semiarid Negeb area that stretched southward toward the desert, the lowlands or foothills between the central hill country and the coastal plain, and the eastern slopes from the highlands toward the Dead Sea.

Another description of the extent of the area subdued is based on its boundaries. Kadesh-barnea was the oasis seventy-five miles south of Hebron. Gaza was on the seacoast, thirty-seven miles west of Hebron. Goshen was probably a border region south of Hebron and Debir, between the southern highlands and the Negeb. Gibeon, so prominent already in the story, marked the northern boundary of this section of Canaan.

The verses do not mean that every single Canaanite was killed—Jerusalem and Gezer continued in enemy hands for decades. However, the back of organized resistance was broken. All that remained were the mopping-up operations by the individual tribes and clans after Joshua died. The scriptural account of the southern campaign is relatively brief, but it makes its point. The Lord had given Israel a decisive, extensive victory. Joshua and his troops were able to return to Gilgal in triumph (v. 43).

Northern (11:1-15)

We have come to the third and final phase of the three-pronged conquest of Canaan. Note that the author's description of the southern campaign was much shorter than the one of the central campaign, and the account of the northern activity is shorter still. Our records are obviously telescoped and selective.

This chapter has the same structural pattern as chapter 10. Its major elements, in order, include the formation of a coalition of the enemy, the Lord's assurance of victory, Joshua's surprise attack, the rout of the enemy, the major enemy cities taken, and a summary of the campaign. The focus is again on one major episode of the campaign. Verse 18 suggests that the overall campaign was much more detailed and extensive.

The military juggernaut of Israel had moved along with rapid and irresistible force. It finally became apparent that it was now or never for any successful resistance. The king of the leading city of northern Canaan was Jabin of Hazor. He formed a hasty alliance that stretched all across the northern section, from the Sea of Galilee to the Mediterranean Sea. It included three cities that are named and several that are not.

The coalition was a powerful one. Not only was it a desperate alliance, with numbers of troops available, but it included many horses and chariots. These relatively advanced forms of military power tipped the odds in favor of the coalition (v. 4).

Hazor is nine miles north of the Sea of Galilee. Madon lay on the heights five miles west of the Sea of Galilee and Shimron the same distance west of Nazareth. Acshaph was located near the south end of the Plain of Acco.

Other kings involved in the coalition are referred to by geographical region. The northern hill country was the highlands of Galilee. Chinneroth was either the Sea of Galilee or a city on its northwestern shore. The Arabah is the Jordan depression south of and perhaps including Chinneroth. The lowland refers to the low hills between the headlands of Carmel and the highlands of Samaria. Naphothdor was the coastal region south of Carmel. Dor was the key city of the area, fifteen miles south of Haifa. Naphoth probably means "the heights" and refers to the foothills of Carmel. The land of Mizpeh probably indicates the valley of Mizpah, a fertile plain either in southern Lebanon or in the upper valley of the Jordan at its source. Mount Hermon is of course the prominent mountain to the north.

Verse 3 is another list of the various ethnic groups in Canaan, almost identical to the lists already encountered. This list makes the alliance extend beyond Galilee, since the Jebusites were in control of Jerusalem. Yes, Jabin's coalition was widespread and formidable. It established its staging point at the waters of Meron, a valley between Hazor and the Sea of Galilee.

Joshua had every reason to be anxious. He must have appreciated the Lord's exhortation not to be afraid and his assurance of immediate and complete victory. Joshua's men would not only be able to win the battle, they would be able to hamstring the enemies' horses and burn their chariots (v. 6). The hamstring is the large tendon back of the horse's hock which, when severed, completely immobilizes him.

As in chapter 10, Joshua used surprise, perhaps after another forced march. The hills and valleys of that part of Canaan are ideal for the type of sudden-strike guerrilla warfare that was Joshua's specialty. The Canaanites probably expected to fight in a more open area where they could make use of their horses and chariots. Joshua got the jump on them and scored another smashing victory. Once again the enemy force was routed and relentlessly pursued in all directions. The account gives the geographical details of this pursuit, to show how complete it was.

Great Sidon is the important Phoenician port of Sidon forty miles to the

north. This reference probably indicates pursuit to the border of its territory. Misrephoth-maim was to the west, on the seacoast. Other pursuit led
northeast toward the valley of Mizpah and Mount Hermon. As always, the
destruction was complete and included both men and war materials (v. 9).

As was his pattern, Joshua next turned his attention to the Canaanite
cities. He attacked first the major city in the north, Hazor. It had been the
most important city between Egypt and the Euphrates River for some five
centuries. It covered two hundred acres and was large enough to accomo-
date 40,000 inhabitants. Joshua killed the king of Hazor and the inhabitants
of the city and burned the city itself with fire. The archaeological records
agree with verses 10-11. Hazor fell sometime between 1250 and 1230 BC.

Other Canaanite cities taken are not named. Nor were their material
goods placed under a complete ban, even though their populations were.
The loot and cattle were made available to the Israelite troops, (v. 14) as we
remember from Ai.

Verse 13 refers to fortified Canaanite cities the Israelites were not able to
take. We see again the indication that the people of Israel settled in the rural
hill country and that much work in completing the conquest remained for
later decades.

Verse 15 is a summary of the northern campaign, and refers to verse 12.
Joshua had been faithful to his commission. He had done what the Lord had
commanded through Moses.

Summary (11:16 to 12:24)

The rest of chapter 11 begins a lengthy summary of the conquest as a
whole. It is a reminder that the basic thrust of the invasion was now complete. All that remained was the long, tedious, and difficult process of root-
ing out isolated pockets of resistance and occupying the land.

Summary of the entire conquest (11:16-23).—Beginning with the south
and moving north, the entire land is described by geographical regions.
This section is very much like 10:40-42, except that it includes all of Palestine (see comments above).

The hill country of verse 16 was the central highlands of Judea. Goshen
was perhaps named for its most prominent settlement. The Arabah was the
entire Jordan Valley including the Dead Sea. The hill country of Israel was
the central highlands north of Judea, particularly the region later occupied
by the tribe of Ephraim.

Verse 17 gives an additional description of the land from the standpoint of its furthest extremes. Mount Halak lay twenty-five miles south-southeast of Beersheba. Seir is a reference to the western edge of Edomite territory. Baal-gad was in the far north, in the land or the valley of Mizpeh, just to the west of Mount Hermon. These southern and northern limits extend slightly beyond the traditional description of Dan and Beersheba.

It is also worth noting that these summary descriptions omit any reference to the coastal plain where the Philistines continued to hold sway or to the Plain of Esdraelon (Jezreel) in the north. Such fringe areas and pockets of resistance defied Israelite control, but the Canaanites were no longer able to offer any organized resistance.

Verse 20 is another common Hebrew way of attributing the victory to the Lord. It was all his doing, including the hardening of the hearts of the enemy so they would resist and be destroyed. It will help us to remember that the Hebrews paid little attention to secondary causes. They tended to downplay human freedom and responsibility. In their view, everything was not just ultimately the activity of God, it was God's doing *directly*. Everything that happened, either good or bad, happened because God caused it. This verse reminds us of such passages as Exodus 4:21, which says that God hardened Pharaoh's heart, even though other passages complete the picture by adding that Pharaoh hardened his own heart (Ex. 8:32).

The Anakim (Josh. 11:21-22) were a tribal group around Hebron that the Hebrews regarded as giants. They were included in the victories Joshua won. We do read later that Caleb and his son-in-law Othniel fought against some of these same people in this same area (15:13-15; Judg. 1:20). Verse 22 also mentions the Philistine cities that remained outside Israelite control.

The last verse of chapter 11 mentions tribal allotments and begins to get us ready for the second major section of the book of Joshua, the allotment and settlement of the land, chapters 13—21. The verse also repeats the reference to Joshua's subjugation of the entire land according to the Lord's instructions through Moses. The Lord had kept his promises to give Israel the land. The war was basically over. The settlement could begin.

The kings of Transjordan (12:1-6).—Chapter 12 provides another type of summary of the conquest, a list of the kings Israel had defeated. We will remember most of them from the stories already studied. However, some of them have not been mentioned in any account so far. The text does not say that all of the cities of these kings were occupied and destroyed. For example, Jerusalem and Gezer lost their kings (10:22-27,33), but neither city was captured by the Israelites until much later.

The chapter begins with a description of the area we call Transjordan, on the eastern side of the Jordan River. The people of Israel defeated the kings listed here when they were still led by Moses. The Arnon Valley formed the southern boundary of this territory. It runs into the Dead Sea, about midway up the eastern side. Mount Hermon was the northern boundary. The Arabah, or Jordan Valley, served as the western edge. The desert lay to the east.

Sihon's kingdom formed the southern part of the region. Heshbon, his chief city, lay twelve miles southwest of the modern capital of the nation of Jordan, Amman. The Jabbok River had its headwaters at Rabboth-ammon (Amman), the Ammonite capital. Gilead was the central highlands of Transjordan. The Sea of Chinneroth is better known as the Sea of Galilee. Beth-jeshimoth lay three miles north of the northeastern corner of the Dead Sea. Pisgah was a peak just northwest of and slightly lower than Mount Nebo.

Og (vv. 4-5) was the other king of this eastern area. Bashan was the fertile tableland east and northeast of the Sea of Galilee. Therefore his kingdom lay north of Sihon's. Ashtaroth and Edrei were his royal cities. The Rephaim, like the Ashtaroth and Edrei were his royal cities. The Rephaim, like the Anakim, were thought of by the Hebrews as giants. Salecah was the eastern border of the kingdom. The Geshurites and the Maacathites formed two small kingdoms, probably just east and northeast of the Sea of Galilee.

Verse 6 reminds us of the defeat of Sihon and Og under Moses, as described in Deuteronomy 2:26 to 3:17. Their territory was given to the two and one-half tribes who settled east of the river, Reuben, Gad, and East Manasseh (Num. 32).

The kings of western Palestine (12:7-24).—The remainder of the chapter is a second list of kings, this time on the western side of the Jordan in Canaan proper. These conquests, of course, were achieved under the leadership of Joshua.

Once again the list is preceded by an outline of the boundaries of the region under consideration. It stretched from Baalgad in the north to Mount Halak in the south and included the central highlands, the Jordan Valley called the Arabah, the slopes between the two areas just mentioned, and the Negeb. The only area mentioned in addition to the lists we saw in 10:40 and 11:16-17 is that the term "wilderness" is added. This is the wilderness of Judea, the arid eastern slopes of the highlands of Judea, between the crest of the hill country and the Dead Sea. It probably included the Negeb region southeast of Arad.

The list of kings in vv. 9-13a is taken from Joshua 6—10, in the same order as that more detailed account. The kings of vv. 13b-16a, whose names we have already encountered, come from chapter 10. They were subdued during the campaign for southern Canaan. However, other kings are cataloged who have not been mentioned previously. Hormah and Arad lay in the Negeb, east of Beersheba. Geder was probably in the same region, but its actual location is unknown. Adullam was in the foothills to the west, in the same area as Libnah and Makkedah.

The kings of vv. 16b-18 came from central Palestine and the coastal plain. Some of them were mentioned in chapter 11. Bethel was the southernmost city in this section. It and Tappuah lay in the hill country of Ephraim. Hepher and Aphek were located on the Plain of Sharon.

Verses 19-23 contain a list of the kings of Galilee (see 11:1). Ta'anach, Megiddo, and Jokeneam were situated along the southwestern border of the Esdraelon (Jezreel) plain. Each one guarded a pass into the plain from the Carmel ridge. Kedesh, the northernmost city the chapter mentions, was in the same general area.

Many scholars think that Lasharon was not the name of a city but rather is connected with Aphek, to distinguish it from other settlements also named Aphek. However, it is necessary to the list if the total is to reach thirty-one (v. 24).

"Goiim in Galilee" (v. 23) is a puzzling expression. The Hebrew text substitutes "Gilgal," four miles north of Aphek. As it appears above, the phrase could be translated "Galilee of the Gentiles" and refers to a group there, perhaps a migrating people related to the Philistines. The area may have been at the foot of Mount Carmel where the plains of Esdraelon and Asher intersect.

Tirzah (v. 24), seven miles northeast of Shechem, was later the second capital of the Northern kingdom of Israel for a brief time.

The area described in vv. 16b-24 lies within the territories of Ephraim and Manasseh in central Palestine. Our material has described no conquest of this area. Many scholars feel this indicates that Israel gained the territory by absorbing distant relatives and sympathizers, thus avoiding open warfare.

The summary of the conquest, as lengthy and detailed as it is, seems to be saying to us: This is it. This is the land, given by God, taken by his command, taken under his direction, and taken by his power. The people have their home; they are ready to begin its settlement.

The Division of the Land
13:1 to 22:34

This begins the second major portion of the book of Joshua. Israelite control had been extended throughout the land, and the apportionment of the various areas and the subsequent settlement could now take place. But the reader should be warned in advance. This second division of Joshua is long and complicated. It is easy to get lost in it as it is little more than a collection of lists of cities and boundaries.

However, it was important to the Israelites. It gave them lengthy and detailed reminders that the Lord had kept his promise to give them the land.

The Territory Yet to Be Conquered (13:1-7)

This brief section introduces chapters 13-21. It begins with the statement that Joshua was old (see 11:8). Israelite influence had been extended throughout all of Canaan, but much land remained to be actually possessed and controlled. Verses 2-6 are a sketch of this territory, basically from south to north.

The Philistines, to the southwest on the Mediterranean coast, had entered the area in a migration from the sea. They had established the five ruling cities listed in verse 3. They gave their name to the entire country, Palestine, and hung on as tenacious enemies of Israel into the days of David.

Shihor originally referred to the Nile River, but here it is east of Egypt. It was a body of water on the Egyptian border, evidently the brook of Egypt of 15:4,47. Its gorge served as the southern border of Canaan. The Geshurites are different from the group named in 12:5, located in Transjordan northeast of the Sea of Galilee. These Geshurites were a tribe of southern Canaan, south of Philistia (1 Sam. 27:8). The Avvim were people to the south and southeast of the Philistine city of Gaza.

Next we move up to north Canaan (vv. 4-6). Unconquered land in the north included much of the modern nation of Lebanon. Mearah, Aphek, and the land of the Gebalites were in the territory of the Phoenicians, who were called by the name of their chief city of Sidon. Aphek is different from the place mentioned in 12:8 and 19:30. It was probably Afka, east of Gebel, at the source of the Adonis River. Gebal was Byblos, or the modern Jebeil, on the coast north of Beruit.

"All Lebanon, toward the sunrising" (v. 5) indicates the great valley between the Lebanon and Anti-Lebanon mountain ranges. Baalgad was the valley below and west of Mount Hermon. "The entrance of Hamath" (v. 5) might also be written "Lebo-hamath." Hamath, or Hama, was an important city-state on the Orontes River. Lebo may have been a city on the southern border of the territory of Hamath. Misrephoth-maim was the western limit of the hill country. It lay south of the coastal landmark called the Ladder of Tyre.

Israel never occupied all of this north country. Her northern most expansion was under David and Solomon when the boundary of the empire reached "the entrance of Hamath" (v. 5; see 1 Kings 8:65; 2 Kings 14:25). The Phoenician coastal cities were able to remain independent. Nevertheless, all the regions named were considered to be a part of what God had promised.

At the conclusion of this list of territories yet to be conquered, the Lord assured Joshua that he himself would drive the inhabitants out before him. With this assurance, he was to go ahead and distribute the various areas, even the unconquered portions. Joshua, who had served so effectively in leading the conquest, was to serve his people in a further capacity by supervising the allotments of territory.

As verse 7 reminds us, only nine and one-half tribes remained who had not received their inheritances. These were the tribes that would settle west of the river.

The Territory of the Tribes East of the Jordan (13:8-33)

Following the introduction just discussed, we begin the actual apportionment of the land among the various tribes. This material reminds us that, despite her victories, Israel was not a united people. She was still a group of separate tribes, and would continue as such for generations. We can see this demonstrated in the fact that each tribe had a territory of its own, claimed its territorial inheritance as a separate tribe, and was responsible for securing and settling it.

The boundaries described in the next several chapters are often poorly defined. The cities and areas listed are too numerous to deal with individually, even if we could always identify them precisely. For other biblical material on this section, see Deuteronomy 2:1 to 3:29.

Survey of the Territory to Be Distributed (13:8-14)

Moses had given Reuben, Gad, and East Manasseh their territory. Again in verse 13 we see the admission that all of the territory allotted had not been completely conquered.

This material is treated in detail in 12:1-6. Two additional places are mentioned here, Medeba and Dibon (v. 9), twenty and forty miles south of Amman, the capital of Jordan, on the main north-south road through the area. Dibon was the royal city of Mesha, king of Moab. It was there that the famous Moabite Stone was found, a significant archaeological discovery.

Maacath and Geshur were Aramean states east and northeast of the Sea of Galilee. David married a daughter of the king of Geshur. He had a son by her and named him Absalom (2 Sam. 3:3).

Verse 14 contains a reminder that the tribe of Levi did not receive a territorial allotment as does verse 33: "The offerings by fire to the Lord God of Israel are their inheritance" (v. 14), and "The Lord God of Israel is their inheritance" (v. 33), as Moses himself had said. Levi was not to be troubled with the tasks of securing a territory and conquering or establishing cities. That tribe was to give all its attention to serving God and his people.

The Territory of Reuben (13:15-23)

The Arnon River formed the northern border of Moab and the southern border of Reuben. The Wadi Hesban, a valley leading from Heshbon to the lower Jordan, lay to the north. The Dead Sea and the Jordan River served as a western boundary. The desert lay to the east. Verse 22 is a passing mention of the false prophet Balaam who troubled Israel during their desert wanderings.

The Territory of Gad (13:24-28)

Gad's inheritance lay in Gilead, the highland area of Transjordan north and south of the Jabbok, in the northern portion of what had been the kingdom of Sihon. Israel had not invaded the land of Ammon (v. 25), but Sihon had, and in conquering him Israel had taken control of much Ammonite land. Rabbah, the Amorite capital, is also called Rabbath-ammon, modern Amman. The cities of verse 26 are located in the eastern highlands and those of verse 27 in the Jordan Valley.

Gad's territory was bounded on the south by Reuben, with the Wadi Hesban as their common border. On the north the inheritance extended into the vicinity of Mahanaim, just across the Jabbok River in the hills of Gilead. Gad also claimed a strip of territory on the east bank of the Jordan as far as the south end of the Sea of Galilee. On the southeast lay Aroer, near Amman.

The Territory of East Manasseh (13:29-33)

The eastern half of the tribe of Manasseh was situated north and east of Gad. This group received half the hill country of Gilead north from Mahanaim, the towns of Jair in Bashan south of the Yarmuk River, and the territory of the kingdom of Og in Bashan east and northeast of the Sea of Galilee. On the west the territory joined Gad's strip along the Jordan Valley. The north and east boundaries were probably the limits of Og's kingdom.

The chapter ends with a summary reminder that these are the inheritances Moses had authorized when the people were still camped on the plains of Moab, waiting to cross the Jordan River.

The Territory of the Tribes West of Jordan (14:1 to 19:51)

Following a brief introduction (14:1-5) and a parenthesis (14:6-15), the account turns to the distribution of western Palestine among the remaining nine and one-half tribes. This lengthy and detailed section will complete the second major division of the book and bring us to its stirring climax.

Introduction (14:1-5)

These verses introduce the entire section about the division of Canaan— we could move from them directly to chapter 15. They remind us of others who participated with Joshua in the actual mechanics of making tribal allotments. Verse 1 indicates the participation of the religious leaders.

Verses 1 and 5 include the tribal representatives who served as political leaders.

Eleazar was the son and successor of Aaron as high priest (Num. 3:32; Duet. 10:6). Numbers 34:16-17 assigns him the role of participating with Joshua in distributing the land grants. The next verse includes the tribal representatives (Num. 34:18). See also Joshua 19:49-51 for information on the participation of these others who served with Joshua.

The Lord's command to Moses (v. 2) is found in Numbers 34:13. We have seen the use of sacred lots before in this book in the story of the exposure of Achan (Josh. 7:14). Another emphasis on lots in the land distribution process comes in 18:2-10.

Verses 2-4 again emphasize that we are talking about only nine and one-half tribes who settled in the western area. Since the tribe of Levi had no territorial inheritance (v. 4), the people of Joseph were divided into two tribes, Ephraim and Manasseh, to restore the original number of twelve. The cities of the Levites mentioned in verse 4 will be dealt with fully in chapter 21.

We might think the chapters to follow to be an overemphasis on the distribution of the land. However, an orderly allocation was of the utmost necessity. Otherwise there might have been excessive competition between larger, stronger, more land-hungry tribes. There would at least have been jealousy over the more desirable portions. The various tribes would thus have weakened each other and left themselves vulnerable to the Canaanites.

The Inheritance of Hebron by Caleb (14:6-15)

Before the individual western tribes are discussed, our text presents a parenthesis relating to a true Israelite hero, Caleb. He is already associated in our minds with Joshua. They were the only adults of the Exodus generation to enter the Promised Land. This section presents him as a worthy pattern for all of God's people.

While the people were still camped at Gilgal, Caleb asserted a special land claim. Verse 6 calls him a Kenizzite. This tribe had descended from Kenaz, a descendant of Esau and thus of Edomite background (Gen. 36:9-11). Since Numbers 13:6 and 34:19 say that Caleb belonged to the tribe of Judah, this is another clear case of the Israelites assimilating an outside tribal group.

These "naturalized" Israelites adopted Israel's culture and religion. In return, they gained full rights in the Israelite community. So here is Caleb, a "foreigner," yet in such a position of honor in Israel. He stood alongside Joshua in some of the most crucial and dramatic times in Israel's early history (Num. 13:30 to 14:10; Deut. 1:34-38). We will see the same thing later with Ruth, the honored ancestress of King David (Ruth 4:13-17).

Caleb began by reminding Joshua of what the Lord had said to Moses when they were still at Kadesh-barnea. He, at age forty, had served with Joshua as one of the twelve spies sent secretly into Canaan. This "foreigner" had been the representative of the tribe of Judah. He and Joshua had returned with the positive, optimistic, minority report. The unfaithful majority of the spies had adversely influenced the people. However, Caleb had "wholly followed the Lord" (vv. 8-9; see Deut. 1:35-36).

Moses had shown to him on that day that he could have a good portion of the land he had helped to spy out. It would be his and his children's on a permanent basis. This would be his reward for remarkable loyalty under the most trying circumstances.

Caleb next pointed out that the Lord had done his part. God had kept him alive and healthy for forty-five more years. Now, at eighty-five and still vigorous and strong, Caleb called on Joshua to do his part by enforcing his claim to the hill country around Hebron. This was one region the spies visited (Num. 13:22; if we compare v. 10 with Deut. 2:14 we get a time frame of five to seven years for the conquest up to this point).

Verse 12 records Caleb's admission that there were giants and strongly fortified cities in the area he was claiming. However, he proposed to take it for his own, not through his own notable strength but because of the Lord's presence.

An old man blessed an older man when Joshua blessed Caleb. Joshua gave him Hebron for his inheritance. His family had continued to inhabit that territory even down to the time when this book was put together, because the noble ancestor, Caleb, had "wholly followed the Lord, the God of Israel" (v. 14).

The final verse of the chapter notes that Hebron had formerly been called Kiriath-arba. The name literally means "city of four." We might call it "four cities," or "four-points." Arba is an unusual proper name here and in 15:13 and 21:11.

What can we say about the story of Caleb? He was a noble figure and a true man of God. His life demonstrates that the Lord keeps his promises to those who wholly follow him. Caleb stood tall as a worthy pattern for the entire nation of what God expects and of the results of obedience.

The Territory of Judah (15:1-63)

The story of Caleb's claim to Hebron leads naturally into the discussion of the land appropriation for his tribe. As we would expect, the priority is given to Judah. Judah's territory is described from the standpoint of its boundaries, the capture of Hebron and Debir by Caleb and Othniel, and the towns in the various administrative districts.

The boundaries of Judah (15:1-12).—Judah received a large apportionment in comparison with the other tribes. However, much of it was desert or near-desert. The boundaries reflect not the territory Judah controlled, but what she claimed.

Not only was Judah's allotment large, it was also diverse. It included hill country, the Negeb in the south, the Arabah to the east, the foothills, and the slopes, as we have seen in 10:40 and 11:16. It also included the southern coastal plain, the Plain of Philistia. Further, Judah's boundaries included the territory of the tribe of Simeon. Simeon was never prominent and rather quickly ceased to exist as a separate tribe.

Judah's southern boundary is given in vv. 2-4 (see Num. 34:3-5). It ran from the southern end of the Dead Sea southwestward to a point below Kadesh-barnea. The ascent of Akrabbim was a pass leading from the Arabah northwest toward Beersheba. From Kadesh-barnea the boundary turned northwestward to the book of Egypt, the usual border between Egypt and Canaan. It followed that stream up to the Mediterranean coast.

The eastern boundary was the Dead Sea (Josh. v. 5). The northern boundary (vv. 5-11) reached from the mouth of the Jordan, northwestward to a point a little south of Jericho, then sharply southward through the valley of Achor. It followed the road from Jericho to Jerusalem and through the valley of Hinnon south of Jerusalem. From there the line ran from the northern end of the valley of Rephaim, roughly along the line of the Jerusalem-Joppa highway to Kirjath-jearim, then southwestward to Beth-shemesh in the valley of Sorek, and northwestward again through the valley past Ekron and Jabneel to the seacoast eight miles south of Joppa.

The Gilgal of v. 7 is a different Gilgal from the permanent Israelite base camp first encountered in 4:19. The Waters of Nephtoah (v. 9) preserve the name of Merneptah, a pharaoh of the Nineteenth Dynasty in Egypt (1235-1227 BC). He left an inscription describing a military campaign in Palestine. It makes the first known mention of the people of Israel outside of the Bible.

The western boundary was the Mediterranean coast (v. 12).

Caleb and Othniel take Hebron and Debir (15:13-19).—The account of Judah's territory is interrupted by reference to the Kennizite clans of Caleb and Othniel, which were affiliated with Judah. Verse 13 serves almost as a conclusion to the story of Caleb's claim to Hebron from the previous chapter (14:6-15). Verse 14 is the realization of the hope expressed in 14:15. Caleb was able to drive out the large and powerful sons of Anak and make Hebron his own.

Next Caleb turned to Debir, then also called Kiriath-sepher. He offered his daughter Achsah as the wife of anyone who helped him in the conquest. She must have been a worthy prize, because Othniel certainly worked hard to win her.

Joshua 10:38-39 refers to the capture of Debir by Joshua. Archaeological research does show that the city was violently destroyed at the end of the thirteenth century. In some places the ashes were three feet thick. It may be that a follow-up assault by Othniel was necessary to complete Joshua's efforts and achieve permanent control.

Othniel was a Kennizite like Caleb. Verse 13 calls Caleb the son of Jephunneh while Othniel is called simply the son of Kenaz. The simplest explanation is that Othniel was Caleb's nephew and also became his son-in-law. "Brother" could mean Othniel was from the same tribe.

Achsah had in mind a worthwhile plot of land for her father to give as a dowry upon her marriage to Othniel. This gift lay to the south and included rare and necessary water. "Springs" (v. 19) literally means "basins" or "bowls," and may refer to reservoirs or cisterns. (See Judg. 1:11-15 for this story in almost identical language).

District town lists of Judah (15:20-63).—The remainder of the chapter is a list of towns. Once again many Bible students feel it was written in light of later times. It presupposes the existence of major cities, each surrounded by satellite-like villages. Related territories assigned to other tribes are discussed in 18:21-28 (Benjamin), 19:2-9 (Simeon), and 19:40-46 (Dan). The Hebrew text has only eleven districts, but the ancient Greek translation of the Old Testament provides the expected twelfth.

We do need to note that verses 45-47 include Philistine cities. Verse 63 is a reference to the invincibility of Jerusalem. Joshua had killed its king in 12:10. Judges 1:8 seems to tell of the capture of the city. But, as Judges 19:10-12 says, it remained a Jebusite stronghold until the time of David (2 Sam. 5:6-10). It lay on the border of Judah and Benjamin (v. 18; 18:16), and was apparently open to both tribes (see Judg. 1:21).

The Territory of the Joseph Tribes (16:1 to 17:18)

There is much less information here than in the previous chapter. There is more duplication, and the information is more approximate and less complete. For example, there are no city lists for the Joseph tribes, despite 16:9. And some of the borders can be understood only with reference to the information on the borders of the neighboring tribes.

The territory of Ephraim (16:1-10).—The description of this allotment begins with the southern border. We find help in understanding this boundary by comparing the adjoining border of Benjamin described in 18:12-13. It ran from the Jordan River near Jericho up the ridge from the wilderness to Beth-aven (more familiar to us as Ai; 18:12) and Bethel. Bethel and Luz are the same (18:13; Judg. 1:23). Ataroth is called Ataroth-addar in Joshua 18:13. The line then moved down the valley past upper and lower Beth-horon into the foothills at Gezer. West of Gezer its course is indefinite as it crossed the coastal plain to the Mediterranean Sea.

The last part of verse 5 also seems to belong with the description of the southern border. It mentions Ataroth-addar (v. 2 and 18:13) and upper Beth-horon.

The eastern boundary of Ephraim began on the north at Taanathshilon, southeast of Shechem, and ran to and down along the western edge of the Jordan Valley to a point just north of Jericho (vv. 6b-7). The record of the northern border is somewhat mixed in with that of the eastern border and can best be understood in light of 17:7-10, the adjoining southern border of West Manasseh. Michmethath (17:7) lay near Shechem. From there the line ran southward to Tappuah (17:7-8) and then westward along the brook Kanah to the sea some three and one-half miles north of Joppa. (The Ataroth of verse 7 seems to be different from the Ataroth of vv. 2,5; 18:13). The western border was of course the Mediterranean Sea.

The final verse of the chapter answers a logical question: Why were there Canaanites still living in the land, even after the immensely successful invasion under Joshua? The tribe of Ephraim was unable to take the city of Gezer, even though it did exercise some dominance over its people (see Judg. 1:29). It is an admission we are familiar with from many previous references.

The territory of Manasseh (17:1-13).—The first verse of this chapter reminds us that Ephraim, Joseph's younger son, always preceded his older brother, Manasseh. The section describing Manasseh's inheritance is longer, but only because it includes stories unrelated to the boundaries or other territorial descriptions.

Manasseh's holdings were on both sides of the Jordan River. The eastern section was made up of Gilead and Bashan, southeast and east of the Sea of Galilee (13:29-31, vv. 5-6). The western area lay between Shechem on the south and the Esdraelon (Jezreel) Plain on the north. The east and west boundaries of West Manasseh were the Jordan River and the Mediterranean.

The six clans of Manasseh (v. 2) are designated as descendants of Gilead in Numbers 26:28-34 and 1 Chronicles 7:14-19. Perhaps some Gileadite clans who conquered the land east of the Jordan were a part of the invasion of western Palestine and were absorbed into this tribe, as Caleb and the other Kennizites were taken into the tribe of Judah. Abiezer was of the clan of Gideon (Judg. 6:11). On Hepher see 12:17, on Tirzah, 12:24. Shechem, Helek, and Tirzah were ancient Canaanite cities.

Verses 3-6 record a fascinating story. The daughters of Zelophehad, who had no brothers, approached Eleazar the high priest and Joshua to make a territorial claim of their own. They traced their assertion of women's rights back to a decision by Moses (Num. 27:1-11; 36:1-12). Joshua granted them a regular inheritance in accordance with Moses' intentions.

The description of the boundaries that begins in verse 7 is vague and incomplete. "From Asher to Michmethath" is more of a line drawn across Manasseh than an actual border description. See 16:6-8 for a discussion of Manasseh's southern boundary, bordering Ephraim. The northern boundary touched the southern edges of Asher (19:24-31), Zebulon (19:10-16), and Isaachar (19:17-23).

Verse 11 indicates that West Manasseh had certain cities in the territories of Asher and Isaachar. These cities were located in the Esdraelon Valley, with the exception of Dor, which lay on the seacoast southwest of Mount Carmel. En-dor is quite far north to be associated with Manasseh. It is omitted from the parallel passage in Judges 1:27.

Bethshean, Ibleam, Taanach, and Megiddo were strong fortress cities. Bethshean guarded the areas where the Esdraelon Valley and the Jordan Valley met. The other three were spaced along the southern edge of the Esdraelon Valley, guarding passes from the hills on the south down into the plain.

Judges 1:27-28 is a parallel to Joshua 17:12-13. These strong fortresses

were able to resist Manasseh. Canaanite Megiddo, for example, fell to Israel
in the last half of the twelfth century, a century after the time of Joshua.
However, the people of Manasseh were eventually able to subject these
Canaanites to forced labor, as in 16:10.

The demand for additional territory (17:14-18).—The account of the
inheritance of the Joseph tribes concludes with a complaint and a challenge.
Here the tribes of Ephraim and Manasseh appeared as one tribe again, as
they did in 16:1-3. They complained about receiving only "one lot and one
portion" (v. 14) in light of the fact that they were so numerous.

Joshua's response was a challenge to clear the wooded areas of their territory. The forest he mentioned was the thinly populated hill country of
Samaria. In verse 16 the Joseph tribes confessed their hesitancy about facing
the Canaanites with their imposing chariots that used iron as armor plating.

Joshua reassured his petitioners that they were so numerous and great
that they would eventually be able to drive out the Canaanites, strong and
well-armed though they were. Once again we see indication that the Israelites initially settled in the hill country and had to leave the plains and
valleys to the land's inhabitants until their own strength grew to the point of
being able to attack the fortified cities.

The Allotments to the Remaining Tribes (18:1 to 19:51)

The first distribution of territory was made to the two and one-half tribes
of Transjordan while the people were still camped on the plains of Moab
(13:32). The second was made to Judah and the two Joseph tribes at Gilgal
(14:6). This third took place at Shiloh (18:1, 8-10). These chapters also give
us more detailed information for the southern tribes of Benjamin and
Simeon. However, none of the sections are so detailed as those of the three
primary tribes who occupied the major part of the hill country.

The remaining land surveyed and divided (18:1-10).—Shiloh was in the
central hill country of Ephraim, ten miles north of Bethel. There the
congregation (v.1) set up the tabernacle and the ark of the covenant. Shiloh
was the central shrine of Israel (22:19,29) until it was destroyed by the
Philistines about 1050 BC, an event probably referred to in 1 Samuel 4.

Seven tribes had not yet received any allotment of land, and Joshua felt
that it was partly their own fault. He scolded them for being lax about going
in and taking possession of what the Lord had already given them (v. 3), as
Judah and the two Joseph tribes had previously done (v. 5).

Joshua took the initiative by requesting a land survey committee composed of three men from each of the seven tribes. These men were to prepare a written description of the land that would form the basis for the division and bring it back to Joshua for the ceremony of sacred lots. This is similar to the childhood practice of settling a dispute by letting one youngster divide the item in question and the other one get first choice of his part. The tribes of Levi, Reuben, Gad, Manasseh, Ephraim, and Judah were specifically excluded from the process (vv. 5,7).

By now we are familiar with this literary pattern: verses 2-7 describe the proposal in detail and verses 8-10 tell how the proposal was thoroughly carried out. In this way the remaining tribes received their inheritances as described through the end of chapter 19.

The territory of Benjamin (18:11-28).—Benjamin received a piece of territory between Ephraim and Judah (v. 11). It is described first in terms of its boundaries (vv. 11-20) and then in terms of the listing of its cities (vv. 21-28).

The northern boundary of Benjamin (vv. 11-13) corresponded to Ephraim's southern boundary (16:1-4). It ran from the Jordan westward to lower Beth-horon. The western boundary (v. 14) ran from lower Beth-horon southward to Kiriath-jearim, on the northern border of Judah. The southern border (vv. 15-19) ran from Kiriath-jearim eastward to the mouth of the Jordan River, a line that also formed the northern border of Judah (15:5-9). The Jordan River itself served as Benjamin's border on the east (v. 20).

The chapter concludes with a list of the cities of Benjamin by geographical district, as in the case of Judah. The first group (vv. 21-24) lay in eastern Benjamin, somewhat overlapping southeastern Ephraim. The second and last group is in verses 25-28.

It is interesting to note that Beth-arabah (v. 22) was given to Judah in 15:5,61 and Kiriath-jearim (v. 28) to Judah in 15:60. Border towns evidently housed people of both adjoining tribes and were claimed by both. The Jebusite city of Jerusalem (v. 28) lay just inside Benjamin's southern border.

The territory of Simeon (19:1-9).—Simeon received a portion of the large area already designated for Judah. It was located around the southern settlement of Beersheba, in the Negeb. Thus the description of Simeon's allotment consists of only a list of towns. Verses 1 and 9 hint at the fact that Simeon soon lost its independent existence as a tribe and was absorbed into the tribe of Judah, probably by the time of the early monarchy.

Most of the towns of vv. 2-8 appear in 15:21-32. They correspond to Judah's District I in the far south. Ether and Ashan (v. 7), however, are in Judah's District IV in the foothills. Verse 6 is a puzzle because it mentions thirteen cities and fourteen are named (see also vv. 15,30,38). Sheba (Shema in 15:26) was probably not counted.

The territory of Zebulun (19:10-16).—The border descriptions of the Galilean tribes (vv. 10-39) are generally brief, incomplete, and vague.

The southern border of Zebulun (vv. 10b-12) moved in two directions from Sarid on the northern edge of the Esdraelon (Jezreel) Plain. It ran from near Jokneam (12:22) on the west to Daberath at the foot of Mount Tabor on the east. The eastern border (v. 13) ran from Daberath north to Rimmon, six miles north of Nazareth. It followed the course of the Iphtahel Valley west southwest of Rimmon to the edge of the coastal plain and southward to the western end of the southern border (v. 11).

The territory of Issachar (19:17-23).—This allotment lay southeast of Zebulun, but the border list is incomplete and extremely difficult to trace specifically. The territory is generally a square, with the southwest corner at Jezreel in the plain north of Mount Gilboa and the northwest corner touching Zebulun's border at Chesulloth (Chisloth-tabor in v. 12) and Daberath. The northern border ran from Tabor (v. 22) to the Jordan River just south of the Sea of Galilee. The south (v. 19) boundary ran from Jezreel east to the Jordan above Beth-shean.

The territory of Asher (19:24-31).—Asher lay generally west of Zebulun. Again, the border is unclear. It extended along the sea north of Mount Carmel, roughly along the edge of the mountains of Galilee to the vicinity of Tyre. Kanah was six miles southeast of Tyre. The towns of verses 29-30 were on or near the coast.

The territory of Naphtali (19:32-39).—Naphtali lay east and north of Zebulun. This border description is no more clear than the previous ones. The southern border joined that of Isaachar from Mount Tabor (Aznoth-tabor in v. 34) and ran to the Jordan (v. 33). From Mount Tabor, the western border ran north (v. 34), then west along the shore of the Sea of Galilee, then north again along the edge of the mountains of Galilee overlooking the Jordan. Most of the towns of verses 35-36 were in the latter area. We cannot identify the northern border, but it must have joined Phoenician territory.

The territory of Dan (19:40-48).—The inheritance of Dan is mentioned in connection with the tribes that settled in Galilee. This is true despite the fact that Dan's original apportionment consisted of a small bit of territory west of Benjamin, between Ephraim and Judah, in the foothills west of Jerusalem.

The boundaries are defined in terms of the boundaries of these neighboring tribes, Judah to the south, Ephraim to the north, and Benjamin on the east. The western boundary was the Mediterranean. The picture we get is of a few Danite towns squeezed in among the neighboring tribes. The towns of verses 41-46 fall partly in Judah's District II (15:33-36) and partly in District V (15:45-47).

But this area was Danite mostly in theory. The people of Dan were unable to take some of this territory and were unable to hold other parts (v. 47; see Judg. 1:34; 18:1-31). The pressure of the Philistines was just too great. Eventually the people of Dan migrated northward to Leshem (Laish), on the headwaters of the Jordan River. They drove out the inhabitants, settled down, and took their place among the tribes of Galilee. Any Danites who remained in the south were evidently absorbed by Judah.

Joshua's inheritance (19:49-51).—This is the conclusion of the entire section on the division of the land, which began in 14:1. The people of Israel gave Joshua the city of Timnath-serah, called Timnath-heres in Judges 2:9, ten miles northwest of Bethel. It was of course located in the heart of the hill country of Joshua's tribe of Ephraim (Num. 13:8). He received it, as Caleb had received Hebron, as a reward for services faithfully rendered.

The Cities of Refuge (20:1-9)

At the end of the lengthy section on the division of territory are two additional and related chapters. They deal with the Levitical cities (21:1-42) and the cities of refuge (vv. 1-9), which were also Levitical cities.

Semitic common law emphasized the sacredness of life. It was a grave matter to take life, even by accident. If you killed someone, even without meaning to, you were guilty of bloodshed and could be immediately executed by the surviving family. The next of kin of the victim had the responsibility for avenging the death. In a tribal society, with no strong central governmental authority, requiring blood for blood safeguarded life. It was a strong deterrent against the taking of life, even carelessly, and is still observed in some Arab villages in Palestine.

However, this practice of blood revenge could also be abused. It could lead to blood feuds. The results could be intense and bloody. The cities of refuge gave protection to someone who had committed involuntary man-slaughter. They were off limits to the vengeful relatives of the deceased. They restrained the practice of blood revenge by giving time for tempers to cool and for the judicial machinery to begin to operate (see Ex. 21:12-14).

"The entrance of the gate of the city" (v. 4) was the open area just inside the city gate. It was the center of the city's social, economic, political, and judicial life throughout the period of the Old Testament.

Note that the cities of refuge gave a haven only in cases of involuntary manslaughter. "Without intent" (v. 3) means in error. "Unwittingly" (v. 3) means without knowing. In such cases, the accused was under the protec-tion of God until the charges could be heard by the elders of the city. These city fathers would consider his request for asylum and his guilt or inno-cence. Ultimately, the congregation would judge his case. If he were guilty, he would be turned over to the avenger. If he was innocent, he could remain in the city until the death of the high priest. Then he could return home without risk. Does having to stay in the city of refuge as long as the high priest lived seem extreme? So was any taking of life.

Be sure to notice that all of these provisions applied just as much to "the stranger sojourning among" the people of Israel (v. 9) as it did to the natu-ral-born Israelite. The foreigner had the same rights to a fair trial before the congregation.

The six cities listed in verses 7-8 were located in the northern, central, and southern parts of the country, three on each side of the river. Kedesh was in the hill country of Naphtali in northern Galilee, near the foot of Mount Hermon. Shechem was the ancient tribal center between the twin moun-tains of Ebal and Gerizim in central Samaria. It lay in what is commonly called the hill country of Ephraim even though it was within the tribal boundaries of Manasseh. Kiriath-arba or Hebron was situated in the hill country of Judah south of Jerusalem.

Bezer lay east of Nebo, at the head of the Dead Sea, in the area assigned to Reuben. Ramoth or Ramoth-gilead lay in northeastern Gilead, at the edge of the eastern desert, twenty-five miles southeast of the Sea of Galilee. Golan is a name we are familiar with in modern times. It lay in Bashan, seventeen miles directly east of the Sea of Galilee.

It is obvious that the cities were located so they would be accessible to the people of all the tribes in all parts of Israel. The next chapter indicates that these cities all contained shrines. We do know that the altar of God pro-vided sanctuary from one's enemies (1 Kings 1:50-53; 2:28). The emphasis on the sanctity of life, the suppression of violence, and the rights of the accused to a fair trial were quite advanced for that day.

Levitical Cities (21:1-42)

The males of the tribe of Levi were set apart for priestly service. They had no territorial inheritance. Being the Lord's priests was their inheritance. However, the Levites did receive towns to live in (14:3-4), with the adjoining pasturelands, scattered throughout the other tribal territories. There they could officiate at the local sanctuaries. When worship was later centralized in Jerusalem, they gravitated there.

The heads of the Levite clans made their claim to Eleazar the high priest, the various tribal heads, and Joshua at Shiloh (18:1,8-10), and reminded them of Moses' command in Numbers 35:1-8. The actual apportionment was made by lot. Forty-eight cities were involved (v. 41), four in each tribe. Manasseh was treated as a single unified tribe. This same list appears with minor variations in 1 Chronicles 6:54-81.

We need to remember that the Levites were not the only ones who lived in these towns. Debir (v. 15) had been captured and settled by Othniel, as we saw in 15:15-19. It is interesting that there are no cities listed for central Judah south of Jerusalem, or in the hill country of central Ephraim, except for Shechem, which was actually located in the territory of Manasseh.

The tribe of Levi was divided into three clans (Ex. 6:16-20), with the second of these clans divided again for a total of four groups. Gershon had been Levi's oldest son (v. 6), but Kohath got the priority treatment because his line included the family of Aaron, the family of the priests. The Kohathites were thus divided into Aaronites and all the rest (vv. 4-5). The third line was that of Merari (v. 7).

The cities of the descendants of Aaron were located in the tribes of Judah, Simeon, and Benjamin (vv. 8-19). The cities of the other Kohathite groups fell within the territory of Ephraim, Dan, and West Manasseh (vv. 20-26). The cities of the descendants of Gershon included those in East Manasseh, Issachar, Asher, and Naphtali (vv. 27-33). Finally, the cities for Merari lay in Zebulun, Reuben, and Gad (vv. 34-40). There is some indication in these latter listings that, like Simeon, Reuben soon began to lose its separate tribal identity and become absorbed into Gad.

Conclusion to the Division of the Land, Occupation (21:43-45)

These verses bring the account of the division of the land full circle. They stress that the Lord's covenant promises had been fulfilled. Israel had defeated her enemies and had come into possession of the Land of Promise. She had been obedient, and the Lord had been faithful. The Promised Land was hers. "Not one of all the good promises which the Lord had made to the house of Israel had failed; all came to pass" (v. 45).

The Tribes of Transjordan Return Home (22:1-34)

This chapter brings to an end the stories of the conquest and of the division of the land. It also tells us much about the religious and national attitudes of Israel at this early time.

The Departure (22:1-9)

These verses fulfill the promise of 1:12-18. The soldiers of the two and one-half eastern tribes had lived up to their responsibilities by assisting their brothers in taking the land. Now they were free to return to their wives, children, and lands (1:14). Joshua sent them away with his blessings.

Joshua summoned the people of Reuben, Gad, and East Manasseh to him at Shiloh (v. 9), confessed that they had met the conditions placed on them by Moses when they had originally requested a homeland east of the river, and commended their faithfulness.

Joshua only cautioned them to take care in observing the law of the Lord given through Moses. They were to love the Lord, walk in his ways, keep his commandments, stay true to him, and serve him with heart and soul (v. 5; see Deut. 5:28 to 6:15). "So Joshua blessed them, and sent them away; and they went to their homes" (v. 6). They returned to their homelands with wealth (v. 8) and the satisfaction that they had done their job faithfully and well.

The Dispute over an Altar (22:10-34)

But what shows every promise of being a simple, direct story quickly turns sour. When the eastern peoples reached the Jordan River, they built a large altar there on the bank. Verse 28 says it was patterned after the altar they had just left at Shiloh. What seems to have been an act of sincere devotion caused extreme misunderstanding on the part of the western tribes; an all-out tribal war was threatened. It was assumed that the altar was a violation of the Deuteronomic law of a single valid sanctuary (Deut. 12:5-14). The people of the nine and one-half tribes immediately began to prepare for battle, not against the remaining Canaanites but against their own people.

Fortunately, the western tribes paused long enough to send a delegation to investigate the situation. They sent eleven men, one from each of the western groups, plus Phinehas, the son of Eleazar the high priest, who was known for his zeal for the Lord and against any tendency toward paganism (Num. 25:6-13). This delegation confronted their eastern brothers with their suspicious charges.

The accusation was treachery (v. 16), the same charge leveled against Achan (see 7:1). The presupposition was that the new altar was an indication of rebellion against the Lord, a turning from their brothers, a turning from true worship, and a turning toward idolatry. The reference to Peor in verse 17 is an indication of immorality and idolatry (Num. 25:1-13).

We see again what a strong sense of corporate identity the people of Israel had at this time (vv. 18-19). They felt such a unity that what one did affected all. They remembered how disastrous their parents' sin at Peor had been: 24,000 people had died in a plague. They remembered the disastrous defeat in the first battle of Ai, all because of one man's sin (v. 20). What would be the extent of God's judgment on the entire nation when two and one-half tribes rebelled? No wonder they were frantic.

Verse 19 seems to indicate a feeling that all other lands but Israel were unclean because they lacked the presence of the Lord. The suggestion is that if their eastern territories were unsatisfactory, the tribes there could cross the river again to claim an inheritance on the western side. This was a confrontation, but it was also a plea to the eastern groups to mend their ways.

Finally, the accused tribes had an opportunity to explain, and they were able to clear up the problem easily and quickly. They began by confessing their faith in the Lord and calling him by three of his primary Old Testament names: The Mighty One, God, and the Lord. They expressed confidence that he knew what was in their hearts and was not so upset as their hot-headed brothers. To show their seriousness, they took a solemn oath in his name(s) that he would not spare them if they had rebelled or broken faith (v. 22).

The crux of their defense was that the altar was for witness, not worship. They had not offered any kind of offering on it. Rather, they had set it up as a continuing testimony to their descendants. They were afraid that in the years to come the idea would arise that the easterners had no part in the

Lord. They were afraid that only the western part of Palestine would be considered the Holy Land (v. 25). And they were right! Their brothers were already hinting at that (v. 33), and the idea grew steadily with the passing years.

The eastern tribes did not want their children cut out of the worship of the Lord (v. 25) or full participation in the life of the nation. Therefore they had built the altar, not for sacrifice but for a memorial. It was a witness (v. 34) between the two groups in the two geographical areas, to their national and spiritual unity (vv. 26-28).

The defense so passionately presented convinced even the rigid Phinehas, as well as the other members of his delegation. He confessed that the Lord was still with his people, unifying them, as indicated by the fact that the accused tribes had not actually committed the treachery they were charged with (vv. 30-31).

The delegation returned home with a report that pleased the people. Everyone blessed God and forgot about the intertribal war that had been so narrowly averted. So the people had rest, not only from their enemies, but also from themselves.

Conclusion and Climax
23:1 to 24:33

These chapters provide more than a noble and notable conclusion to the book of Joshua: they provide its climax. They are crammed with importance. They help bring the book full circle, and help prepare us for the book of Judges, especially chapters 2—3.

Joshua's Farewell Address (23:1-16)

It was common, in that part of the world at that time, for the leader of a family or a nation to give parting words, pronounce a blessing on his descendants or followers, and even add curses on his personal or tribal enemies. His words provided guidance for the future for those who were to continue.

This is what Joshua did here. Many years had passed. He was near the

close of his life (vv. 1-2; see 13:1). He called together an assembly of representative officials. His address strikes all the significant notes of the book. He
especially emphasized the Lord's fulfillment of the promises of 1:1-9. He
also stressed the conditional nature of God's grace: God would continue to
bless them if they continued to be obedient.

Joshua's words highlight four primary themes: historical references; the
obligations of the covenant; the blessings that go with faithful obedience;
and the consequences that follow unfaithfulness. The first three parts of this
fourfold pattern appear in verses 3-8 and again in verses 9-11. The final
point is dealt with in verses 12-13. Verses 14-15a are a summary of the
Lord's promises fulfilled and blessings given. The remaining verses are
another strong challenge regarding the consequences of disobedience.

Joshua reminded the leaders and through them the nation that they
themselves had witnessed all that God had done to their enemies. He had
fought for Israel. He had won the victory, not they. He had given them
abnormal strength (vv. 9-10). The territories that had been assigned to the
various tribes had been inhabited by people the Lord had cut off. What is
more, the Lord would continue to give them the areas that were not yet
under their control. He would continue to fulfill his promises *if* they continued to be faithful in keeping what was written in the law (vv. 3-6).

Joshua counseled his people to particularly avoid marriages with unbe-
lievers. These mixed marriages with people who worshiped other gods could
bring nothing but disaster (Deut. 7:3-4). They were not to mention the
names of the gods of the Canaanites left among them, swear by them, serve
them, or worship them. Instead, they were to stay true to the Lord their
God (vv. 7-8,12).

Verse 11 contains an important emphasis that is relatively rare in the Old
Testament: love for the Lord. Their strict obedience to God's commandments was to grow out of their love for him. If their love failed, and conse-
quently their actions, and they turned in the direction of the pagans left
among them, the Lord would allow their enemies to remain in the land to
afflict Israel until she herself perished (vv. 12-13). It was at this point that
Joshua became very blunt and specific.

Joshua confessed again his realization that he was about to die. He
reminded the leaders of the people of how they owed everything to the
Lord, who had surely kept his promises (v. 14). But that divine faithfulness
worked two ways, Joshua insisted. Neither would all the promised evil fail,
if the people turned away from the Lord. His anger would be kindled
against them. He would destroy them in Canaan just as surely as he had

enabled them to invade it successfully, if they transgressed his covenant and turned to false gods (vv. 15-16).

So Israel stood between good and evil. The good meant life, the evil death. The Lord who had fought for them would continue to fight for them until the land was fully won and the nation was permanently established. Disloyalty would bring curses in equal measure. Joshua insisted that the people be aware of the options, and choose.

The Renewal of the Covenant at Shechem (24:1-28)

The final chapter of Joshua is a great and inspiring record of a pivotal event. God's covenant with his people was not automatic. It had to be accepted and followed by each new generation. Once again Joshua showed his superior leadership ability, this time not as a soldier but as a spiritual leader (vv. 29,31).

Joshua gathered the people to the ancient sacred city of Shechem (see Gen. 12:6-7). It lay at the east end of the valley between the twin mountains of Ebal and Gerizim. The Old Testament records no Israelite conquest of Shechem. It may be that the people there were related to the Hebrews and joined them in this covenant relationship with their God. We do know that the Israelites worshiped at Shechem from the early days of the conquest.

As the people and their leaders assembled, they were conscious that they were coming before the Lord (v. 1). Joshua led them through the basic elements of covenant renewal that were common to the ancient world.

God's Blessings on Israel (24:1-13)

Ancient covenant ceremonies began by naming the king or ruler who was the author of the covenant. Joshua did this in verse 2. Then he recalled for the people the grace of the Lord as demonstrated in his providential leadership and actions in their behalf. The repeated demonstrations of God's care placed the people under obligation to be loyal to him.

Verses 2-4 deal with the time of the patriarchs. They originally came from Mesopotamia. Their ancestors had served other gods. But God called Abraham from that polytheistic setting, led his migration to Canaan, and gave him descendants. His grandson Esau received the territory beyond Judah south of the Dead Sea. Jacob went to Egypt.

The next three verses recall the deliverance from Egypt so closely associated with Moses, Aaron, and the plagues (vv. 5-7). At one point darkness protected the fleeing ex-slaves from their former masters (Ex. 14:19-20). The people were able to cross the sea in safety, but their pursuers were destroyed. Thus they escaped into the desert.

God's grace was shown in Transjordan (vv. 8-10) by the defeat of the Amorite kings Og and Sihon. He also protected them against the schemes of Balak and his hired prophet, Balaam. God repeatedly turned Balaam's curses into blessings.

Verses 11-13 conclude the historical review with a summary of God's grace as seen in the occupation of Canaan. With God's guidance and help, the people were able to cross the Jordan, take Jericho, and defeat the various peoples of Canaan. God gave the land and its inhabitants into their hand.   The reference to the hornet in verse 12 is generally taken to indicate the terror that paralyzed the Canaanites as they faced Israel. The term could be translated "panic." That was only one of the ways the Lord gave Israel a land they had not labored for, cities they had not built, and vineyards and oliveyards they had not planted (v. 13). It is obvious that the Old Testament, like the New, is a book of God's grace.

Joshua's Challenge to the People (24:14-15)

The next step in an ancient covenant ceremony had to do with the people's covenant obligations. The record is brief about this point at Shechem. It centers on the people's primary obligation of absolute loyalty. "Fear the Lord," Joshua urged, "and serve him in sincerity and in faithfulness' (v. 14).

Of course, this relationship of loyalty was exclusive. God alone had to be the Lord of all. Therefore the people had to put away all other gods. They had to turn their backs on the gods of Mesopotamia, Egypt, and Canaan (vv.14-15,23). Were the Israelites actually serving such gods at this time? It doesn't seem likely. However, remember that they were periodically taking in new peoples who allied themselves with them and accepted the Lord as their God. Remember also that the Israelites faced the constant temptation of idolatry. Joshua's challenge was timely and well-made.

Notice how much of an emphasis Joshua placed on free will. Both the Lord and the people had to choose—they had to choose each other. Of course, the Lord had clearly demonstrated his choice. He had long ago selected Israel to be his people and had repeatedly backed up that choice with action.

But in turn Israel had to choose him. The choice their fathers had made was not enough. This new generation had to decide, too. They were free to reject the Lord and his covenant, but Joshua urged them to choose the God who had already chosen them.

You have to serve somebody, Joshua so much as said. Go ahead and make up your mind who it will be. But Joshua also knew the importance of a definite positive example. He must have stirred his hearers as he still stirs us who read his words: You do what you think best, but my family and I are going to serve the Lord!

Israel's Declaration of Allegiance (24:16-24)

The people were quick to respond—Joshua thought too quick. Almost before they thought, they affirmed that they would not forsake the Lord to serve other gods. They picked up on the historical review Joshua had given them. They confessed their knowledge that the Lord had been the one who had brought them out of the bondage of Egypt, delivered them with great signs, and preserved them all along their difficult way. He had protected them in the face of their enemies and had driven out the Amorites who lived in the land. "Therefore," the people said, "we also will serve the Lord, for he is our God" (v. 18).

Joshua was not satisfied. He was too wise to accept a hasty, shallow profession that might be temporary or partial. He challenged the people again. He made the decision as difficult and meaningful as he could. He expressed reservations about their sincerity. He pointed out the difficulty of properly serving God. He is holy. By his very nature he is set apart from man. Sinful man cannot stand before him. God is jealous. He will not put up with any rival. He will not forgive, Joshua said, if you turn back to worship foreign gods. Rather, he will destroy you (vv. 19-20).

Perhaps more soberly and deliberately this time, the people reaffirmed their commitment to the covenant. They voluntarily and enthusiastically insisted that they *would* serve the Lord. Joshua observed that they would be held to their decision. He called them witnesses against themselves, and they agreed: "The Lord our God we will serve, and his voice we will obey" (v. 24).

The Covenant Ceremony Concluded (24:25-28)

Satisfied at last, Joshua completed the covenant ceremony. He specified the statutes and ordinances, evidently the detailed provisions of the covenant. Furthermore, he prepared a record of the covenant. Ancient covenant records were generally placed in the sanctuary and read publicly on a regular basis.

Joshua also set up a great stone under the oak in the sanctuary of the

Lord. This stone was to be both a memorial and a witness. Perhaps it came to be a symbol of the Lord's presence. It was a further bind upon the people as they looked back on what they had done. Then Joshua sent the people home.

Significant Deaths and Burials (24:29-33)

With the invasion brought to a successful conclusion, the land distributed, and the covenant officially renewed, Joshua's work was done, and done well. He could accurately be called by the noble title that had been applied to Moses: "The servant of the Lord" (v. 29). It was a sort of Hebrew Congressional Medal of Honor. He died at 110, an age the Egyptians considered to be ideal.

The people buried Joshua in the land they had given him at Timnath-serah in Ephraim. But their most fitting memorial to their fallen leader was the faithful lives they lived. They had served the Lord all of Joshua's life, and they continued to do so during the lives of all the members of Joshua's generation (v. 31; see Judg. 2:7-9). Joshua could truly rest in peace.

Joseph had died in Egypt decades before. However, he had not been buried there. His remains had been mummified and had been taken from Egypt with the Hebrews during the Exodus. When the conquest was completed Joseph's bones were buried at Shechem, in a plot of ground Jacob had bought there for an undetermined sum (Gen. 33:19).

Eleazar also died. He was Aaron's son and successor as high priest. He, too, was buried in a family tomb. And so the book ends by telling us that loose ends had been tied up and, more importantly, key leaders of the nation were passing off the scene. They left a legacy of faithful service to God, but how would the people honor that legacy?

JUDGES

Introduction

The book of Judges is the second book of history in our English Bibles, the second of the Former Prophets according to the Jewish designation. Like Joshua, its name comes from its main characters. It is primarily a collection of stories of some of Israel's early heroes.

Judges is also often called the second book of Deuteronomic history. The books of Joshua through 2 Kings relate the history of Israel from a Deuteronomic or prophetic standpoint. They view life in a way we find in great prophetic books such as Amos, Hosea, and Isaiah: the Lord is the God of history; he is active in history and is carrying out his purposes in history; history is the stage where God rewards the faithful and judges the disobedient, both nations and individuals; if Israel sinned, she was sure to be punished; deliverance would come only if she repented. This Deuteronomic theology of history is best seen in 2:6 to 3:6. The rest of the book is a collection of illustrations—and some of the best stories in any literature.

Joshua generally deals with the great sweep of the invasion and basic conquest, although it gives repeated indication that much work of consolidation remained to be done. Judges, however, presents in detail the painfully slow, tribe-by-tribe efforts to complete the subjugation of Canaan and make the necessary transition to a completely new way of life.

The Who, the When, and the How

Judges gives no hint of an author or time of writing. Several references indicate that it was written during the period of the kings (17:6; 18:1; 19:1; 21:25), so most people place its writing in the time of the united kingdom or just after. Most Bible students are confident of its basic historical accuracy.

The author used the literary device of the cycle to express the truths he wanted to convey. Over, over, and over again the writer illustrated the pattern of sin, judgment, repentance, and deliverance. The people went away from the Lord and were duly punished by the attack of an enemy. After suffering God's judgment for an extended period they saw the error of their ways, repented, and began to cry out to the Lord for deliverance. The Lord responded by raising up a hero—in one case a heroine—to deliver them from the oppressor.

This cycle is the essence of the book. You can see how well it illustrates the truth that the Lord is the God of history and reveals himself through history. It is also an excellent vehicle to convey the Deuteronomic—and prophetic—truth that loyalty is rewarded but disloyalty is severely punished.

The Tribal League

The covenant renewal ceremony at Shechem (Josh. 24:1-28) has been called the Continental Congress for Israel. This is an apt analogy, because Israel after Joshua was very much a confederation. Do you remember learning about the Articles of the Confederation? In the early days of our country, before the Constitution, the colonies formed a loose confederation, without a strong central government.

Similarly, the twelve-tribe league was a confederation of distinct tribes. It was a loose—we would say weak—political structure. The tribes voluntarily aligned themselves for common defense and worship. They had a common language, a common background of customs, and a common sense of law and decency; but they were held together more by religious than by political or social forces. The tribes were separated by geography—by rivers and hills, by the various difficulties each faced, and by preoccupation with meeting their own needs.

The temporary judges and various tribal representatives were the only human leaders. The Lord was the actual head of the nation. The surrounding nations were monarchies, but the Lord was Israel's king. The tribes were bound together because of their covenant with him. God's sanctuaries at different times were at Shechem, Shiloh, Bethel, and Gilgal, with the first two by far the most important. Of course, the tabernacle and the ark of the covenant were at Shiloh.

The period of the judges has been called the Dark Ages of Hebrew history. It was a period of anarchy, intermittent fighting, idolatry, and immorality. The people of this book were often bloodthirsty, cruel, and violent, even while they were showing courage, faithfulness, and integrity. The judges themselves were sometimes guilty of lying, murder, hatred, and immorality. There is little indication that the people were even aware of the law of Moses, much less that they kept it. It is remarkable that the worship of the Lord even survived. It was the utter confusion of the period, together with the threat posed by better organized enemies like the Philistines, that helped push Israel in the direction of a more centralized government (Judg. 17:6; 21:25).

The Judges in Judges

After Joshua died, no strong leader arose to take his place. One-man rule was over for a time; it was not practical when the tribes went in different directions. But Israel did have leaders during this time. Who were these transitional figures who bridged the gap between the one-man rule of Moses and Joshua and the one-man rule of the monarchy, and what did these leaders do?

The meaning of the term.—Our English word *judge* has little connection with the leaders of this book and what they did. Our word means "one who decides or renders a verdict." It suggests a dignified figure in a black robe sitting behind a large desk in a courtroom, handing down legal decisions.

The Israelite judges did have something of a judicial function. They acted as judges in legal disputes (4:4; 10:1-3; 12:7-14). The Hebrew term, however, basically means "deliverer" or "savior." Judges were those who ruled or set things right. They delivered people from their oppressors. They delivered wronged persons, especially those not strong enough to obtain justice on their own.

The judges were civil and political leaders, but they were military champions especially. They were gallant fighters, usually against heavy odds. Of course, they did not usually lead their men against the enemy in formal battlefield encounters. Rather, they staged raids in guerrilla-type fashion, or else they engaged in individual acts of courage and strength.

But how were these dynamic leaders chosen? How did they come to office? They came by the Lord's doing. There is considerable emphasis in Judges on the Spirit of the Lord. These judges were Spirit-controlled leaders. They were gifted by the Lord's Spirit. They were charismatic leaders, in the biblical, not the modern sense. They had the spark of leadership. They were empowered by the Lord (3:10; 6:34; 15:14).

These judges were not elected. They moved to the front because the Lord's Spirit was on them. They were also temporary leaders. They usually served during the emergency, and then retired from the scene. Some, like Samson, served for longer periods. The office was not hereditary. Their sons did not follow them in it. They were common people who returned to obscurity after they had completed their work of deliverance.

Apparently the fame, feats, and evident wisdom and discernment of the judges led people to consult them in cases of legal dispute. This function was secondary, however. Their primary role was that of appearing when trouble threatened and leading the people in relieving the pressure in that particular area.

There are parallels between these judges and the lawmen of the Old American West. Both had a quasi-judicial function. More importantly, they were leaders in unsettled, frontier times. They were individualists. They stood for the right, with occasional lapses. They worked to right wrongs and deliver the oppressed.

The relationship of the judges.—At first glance, Judges reads as if one judge followed another, single file and in sequence, and their various administrations extended over a total period of 410 years. This does not include the years of the two generations following the death of Joshua (2:10). However, there is indication in Scripture that we are not to understand the numbers in this fashion.

First Kings 6:1 lists a total of 480 years from the Exodus to the building of the Temple in Solomon's fourth year, around 956 BC. But if we take the entire 410 years for judges, this would leave only seventy years for the wandering in the desert, the conquest, the period of Eli and Samuel, and the reigns of Saul and David. And that would be handling the chronology of Judges in the fashion of the twentieth century AD, not the eleventh century BC.

It is evident that the emergencies to which the judges responded were regional emergencies. The enemy afflicted a single tribe, and that tribe repelled him, perhaps with the help of one or two others. Apparently only Deborah made war on a more national scale, with several tribes participating. While the preface to each story seems to be phrased in more national terms, it evidently refers to a portion of the nation. Thus some of the judges were contemporaries whose terms overlapped. We also note that many numbers in Judges are expressed in round figures: twenty, forty, eighty, etc.

It is still true that the order of the book is roughly chronological. The book records twelve judges in all, six major and six minor. The accounts of the major judges are long and involved. The minor judges receive so little attention that they remain merely names. But these are the people who stepped to the front in times of danger, gave personal leadership, and rallied the tribes to the battle and to the Lord.

The Times of the Judges

This book covers the period from the death of Joshua to the birth of Samuel. There is general agreement as to dates: 1200 to 1020 BC, most of the twelfth and eleventh centuries. But what was going on in Israel and in neighboring countries at that time?

For Israel.—The period of the conquest was over, and the process of settling into Canaan had begun. Israel faced the long task of completing the initial successful invasion and consolidating the initial settlements. They had destroyed some of the native inhabitants and assimilated others, but pockets of Canaanite resistance remained for centuries. The Jebusites in Jerusalem and the Philistines on the coast were not subdued until the reign of David.

There seems to have been an uneasy accommodation to this situation. The book of Judges records only a single story of open warfare with native inhabitants, under Deborah. Israel had much more trouble with surrounding nations such as Edom, Moab, Ammon, and various nomadic groups from the desert. These foreigners from the fringes made frequent invasions into areas under Israelite control.

But the greatest adjustment Israel had to make was a more subtle one. She had to make the transition from nomadic life in the desert to settled agricultural life on small farms. This transition brought Israel into direct contact with the culture of the Canaanites, and it brought the faith of the Lord into direct confrontation with the cult of Baal.

These new farmers naturally wanted their soil to be fertile and their crops, flocks, and herds productive. They wanted good weather. The fertility cult of Canaan was an acute temptation. The Canaanites insisted that their gods controlled fertility and kept the cycle of the seasons moving properly, and, moreover, the sexual activity of Baal, which means "lord" or "owner," and his female consort, Ashtoreth, made all these things possible. Ritual sexual activity on the part of the disciple of Baal was thought to influence the gods, so the Canaanites staffed their shrines with sacred prostitutes, both male and female. They generally worshiped at high places on the tops of hills. They set up stone pillars or images of the bull, both of which represented Baal, and wooden poles to represent Ashtoreth. They celebrated the death and resurrection of Baal in the changing seasons.

Many Israelites came to look upon the Lord as the God of the desert and of battle, and Baal as the god of agriculture. They felt that both were needed. Perhaps, they thought, one was served by the official and public religion, the other by the more private religion of the home and the farm. These Israelites probably convinced themselves that they were not really forsaking the Lord. They were merely adding some fertility practices to his worship.

But remember that the Lord is a jealous God. To limit him to one sphere and to recognize any other god in any other sphere was a violation of the covenant. We can see how crucial all this was when we look at verses such as 2:10. After the death of Joshua and his generation, a new generation arose that did not know the Lord and had not been eyewitnesses to what he had done for Israel. This new situation reminds us that faith cannot be transferred from one generation to another like a spiritual bank account. To know the Lord means to know him personally, to enter into a personal relationship with him. Each new generation, then and now, must either renew the covenant or repudiate it. The new generation in Israel was in constant danger of doing the latter. It is also true that the downfall of any people begins on the inside. First there is internal, moral, and spiritual decay. Then and only then is there an external danger. The old observation is that nations aren't killed—they commit suicide.

For the other nations.—Mighty Egypt was mighty no longer after the collapse of the Nineteenth Dynasty. She was weak internally and externally. Her control over the surrounding areas such as Canaan loosened and then disappeared. The book of Judges doesn't even mention Egyptian intervention. The Israelites had a breathing spell to establish themselves in their new land.

We learn from Scripture, and confirm from archaeology, that the Canaanites maintained control of the valleys and plains. The period of extended Egyptian weakness allowed the nations on the fringes to begin to flex their muscles, and the desert tribes to extend their range.

The most serious threat to Israel, however, came relatively late. Sea peoples we call Philistines invaded Palestine by both sea and land around 1175 BC, about half a century after the climax of the Israelite invasion. They overwhelmed the Hittites to the north, and the Canaanites, and even invaded Egypt before they were defeated there.

The Philistines competed with the Phoenicians for control of the sea trade. In the middle of the twelfth century they began to penetrate inland. Worst of all, they had a monopoly over the manufacture of iron. They were more than a thorn in Israel's side; they were a deadly foe. They appeared late in the period of the judges and troubled Israel grievously well into the period of the monarchy. In fact, the difficulty of consolidating their tribal territories and defending themselves against better armed and better organized enemies such as the Philistines gradually pushed Israel toward a more centralized form of government. Not even Samson could permanently defeat the Philistines; perhaps a king like Saul could.

The Invasion and Settlement of Canaan
1:1 to 2:5

Judges begins with a sketch of the conquest and occupation of Canaan that emphasizes the efforts of some of the individual tribes. Much of the material parallels the account beginning in Joshua 10. However, it is interesting that Joshua's military leadership is not mentioned in the Judges account. This record takes the viewpoint of the foot soldier who did the actual fighting, not the general who directed it.

The Fortunes of Various Tribes (1:1-36)

The emphasis of this introduction to Judges is on the tribe of Judah. We can tell this by the position and length of the Judah narrative. This is why some people feel Judges was written from a southern viewpoint, and Joshua from a northern point of view. (Joshua was of the tribe of Ephraim, a northern tribe.)

Conquests of Judah and Simeon (1:1-21)

Many people have noted the first phrase of Judges and called it a virtual title for the book. See similar expressions at the beginning of Joshua, 2 Samuel, and 2 Kings. Since Joshua's death is so heavily stressed, beginning in 2:6, the phrase here is probably a way of introducing the book and setting the stage for the book as a whole. The events described in chapter 1 evidently took place during Joshua's lifetime.

Israel was still camped at Gilgal, the original camp in Canaan (Josh. 4:19), but the tribal allotments had already been made. As was customary in those days, the people inquired of the Lord before launching a military campaign. They probably did this through their national leaders by means of casting a sacred lot. The Lord's response indicated that Judah should act first, and, with Simeon, he moved against the Canaanites in the Jerusalem area. Notice that the tribes are spoken of as individual men.

The Canaanites who were defeated included the Perizzites, a name referring either to a certain group of people or more generally to those who lived in unwalled towns. Of course, credit for the victories belonged to the Lord (Judg. 1:4). In fact, verse 2 records the Lord speaking as if the deed was as good as done, as if he had already accomplished it.

Events in verses 3-8 are also related in Joshua 10:1-27. Both tell of a campaign in southern Palestine against Canaanite forces, the capture of the cities of Hebron and Debir, and probably the same enemy king who is associated with Jerusalem. But there are differences in the accounts, probably because of different purposes and different viewpoints. For instance, the name of the enemy leader is different. Here it is Adoni-bezek.

Adoni-bezek's army was defeated, and, when he fled, he was captured. He was mutilated in the same way he had mistreated a number of his own enemies (Judg. 1:6-7). This not only incapacitated an enemy, it was an act of humiliation. Some such victims scavenged for scraps under their conqueror's table. It made the man unfit for military and perhaps also religious leadership. Adoni-bezek's men carried him back to Jerusalem to die.

Verse 8 describes the capture and burning of Jerusalem, but verse 21 reminds us that the Jebusites continued to control the city (see Josh. 15:63). Jerusalem was evidently taken more than once, as were many other sites during this same time. Or perhaps a Jebusite stronghold on Mount Zion survived Israel's attack, with the rest of the urban areas captured and burned but soon retaken.

There were further campaigns by Judah into the central highlands south of Jerusalem, the dry country called the Negeb that bordered the desert, and the foothills between the highlands and the Philistine Plain. Hebron (v. 10) was the highest point in the hill country. Debir and Zerphath or Hormah (vv. 11,17) lay in the Negeb, and Gaza, Askelon, and Ekron (v. 18) in the foothills.

Hebron was eighteen miles south of Jerusalem. It was originally called Kiriath-arba after Arba, the father of Anak. Sheshai, Ahiman, and Talmai were descendants of Anak, according to Joshua 15:14. These Anakim of the southern hill country were a populous tribe of large stature. Joshua 11:21-23 says that Joshua wiped them out. Joshua 15:13-19 and Judges 1:20 attribute their defeat and the capture of Hebron to Caleb, whose Kenizzite clan formed a part of the tribe of Judah. Judges 1:10 mentions only the tribe of Judah.

The next target, Debir or Kiriath-sepher, lay eleven miles southwest of Hebron on the edge of the Negeb. It was captured by Othniel, Caleb's nephew, who received Caleb's daughter Achsah as a prize for his victory. Achsah in turn asked her father for a well-watered portion of southern land as a part of her dowry (see Josh. 15:15-19).

The Kenites mentioned in verse 16 were smiths who lived in the Negeb before the Israelites entered Canaan. They were related to the Amalekites but had been friendly with Israel since Moses married into the clan (1 Sam. 15:6). They, too, became an element of Judah and assisted in the conquest. They settled near Arad, fifteen miles south of Hebron. Note their relationship with the previous inhabitants (Judg. 1:16).

Zephath, twenty miles southwest of Hebron, was the only city placed under the sacred ban of total destruction. Its name was changed to Hormah, which means "devoted" or "placed under the ban."

The ancient Greek translation of 1:18 says that Judah *did not* take the Philistine cities of Gaza, Askelon, and Ekron. (See also v. 19.) And no wonder. Though Judah could secure the hill country, the Canaanites and Philistines had chariots overlaid with iron armor. The Israelites were lightly armed by comparison. The enemy retained control of the fertile valleys and plains. But the picture of Israel gradually moving down the hills into the valleys is exactly the picture archaeological research gives us.

Conquests of the Joseph Tribes (1:22-29)

The Joseph tribes of Ephraim and Manasseh moved against Bethel, in the central highlands north of Jerusalem. They took the city by subversion. The spies they sent made contact with a citizen and struck a bargain with him (vv. 22-25), similar to that earlier spies had made with Rahab. They asked him to show them a secret way into the city, perhaps through a water tunnel from the city to a spring. The city was easily taken, and the man and his family were spared. The land of the Hittites is a reference to northern Syria, then under Hittite control. The location of Luz is unknown. As for Bethel, it became an important sanctuary (Judg. 20:26-28).

Pockets of Canaanite resistance remained in the area, often in fortified cities (see Josh. 17:7-13). Ephraim and Manasseh were hemmed in on both the north and south by Canaanite fortresses that stretched in an almost straight line from the Jordan Valley to the Mediterranean. These fortresses were strategically located, well-populated, and able to resist Israelite attack.

Beth-shean guarded the juncture of the Jordan and Jezreel Valleys. Taanach and Megiddo controlled the passes from the Sharon Plain to Esdraelon. Dor lay on the coast just south of Mount Carmel. Ibleam guarded the road from Bethel and Shechem to Esdraelon. Gezer was eighteen miles west of Jerusalem, at the southwestern corner of Ephraim's territory. It was not conquered until the days of Solomon (1 Kings 9:15-17). The Canaanites continued to live in the land, but whenever Israel was strong enough, she put them to forced labor (Judg. 1:28).

The Situation of Other Tribes (1:30-36)

Verses 27-36 deal almost exclusively with the peoples the Israelites did not conquer. Since no battles are recorded, there was evidently a largely peaceful settlement of the area. But there were also many Canaanites left virtually unchallenged.

Zebulun (v. 30) was located in north central Palestine somewhat south of the Sea of Galilee. Kitron and Nahalol have not been identified. Asher (vv. 31-32) had a coastal strip some ten miles wide from Mount Carmel north to Ahlab. Asher left more unconquered cities than any other tribe. The territory of Naphtali (v. 33) ran from Mount Tabor north to Upper Galilee, and from Asher to the headwaters of the Jordan.

The positioning of Dan in verses 34-36 predates the northern migration described in chapters 17—18. The Philistines drove the Amorites northward into Dan and forced them from the foothills up into the hill country. *Amorites*, or *Westerners*, is here a synonym for *Canaanites*. Aijalon was in the hill country eleven miles northwest of Jerusalem, but, though Dan was originally in the center of Palestine, it never established its position there.

The Explanation of the Presence of the Canaanites (2:1-5)

This paragraph gives the explanation for the continued presence of the Canaanites, but gives it from the divine point of view, whereas other verses have given it from the human perspective. A divine appearance occurred in some perceptible form. The angel of the Lord (v. 1) was in this case a close representative of God himself. Notice that he spoke for God and even spoke God's words (vv. 1-3).

God, through his messenger, reminded the people of his grace in delivering them from Egypt, guiding them into the Land of Promise, and establishing with them an unbreakable covenant. He affirmed his faithfulness to the covenant by asserting, "I will never break my covenant with you" (v. 1). However, he said, the people had disobeyed his command to avoid covenants with the inhabitants of the land. They had also permitted pagan altars to continue to stand.

This indication of their disobedience would also become a part of their punishment. The Lord would not drive out the native inhabitants. Instead, these peoples would become Israel's enemies in many future battles and their gods a snare to God's people (Josh. 23:13).

The people were moved to contrition by the Lord's message. They wept aloud. In fact, they named the place Bochim, "Weepers." There they worshiped by offering sacrifices to the Lord. There is no record of a response from the Lord.

Some people identify Bochim with Bethel. They see in this report a transfer of the religious center of Israel from Gilgal, the first Israelite camp in Canaan, to Bochim, after the invasion was partially accomplished. The section also indicates that the order of the day would be the assimilation of some of the Canaanites, not their annihilation or expulsion.

Israel Under the Judges
2:6 to 16:31

We come now to the heart of the book. These fifteen chapters are what usually come to mind when someone mentions Judges. After an introduction of approximately one chapter in length (2:6 to 3:6), each judge is dealt with separately, some in a sentence or two, some in a paragraph, and some in multiple chapters.

During the Time of Joshua and Afterwards (2:6 to 3:6)

This summary of the situation in Canaan after the conquest is the account of the new generation, its apostasy, and the Lord's response of judgment. It gives a framework for the stories of the ancient heroes and comprises a transition from the story of the conquest to the actual stories of the judges.

Joshua's Last Years and Death (2:6-10)

If we were to omit Judges 1:1 to 2:5, verse 6 would take up where Joshua 24:28 ended and continue in fine fashion. Judges 2:6-10 repeats Joshua's obituary with only slight variations. In this case his burial city is called Timnath-heres rather than Timnath-serah (Josh. 24:30). It was fifteen miles southwest of Shechem, at the foot of Mount Gerash.

The people of Israel served the Lord faithfully all the days of Joshua and his contemporaries. However, the members of the younger generation had not been firsthand witnesses to the mighty acts of God in history as had their forebears. Thus they were more readily tempted by the agricultural gods of Canaan.

The Situation After Joshua's Death (2:11 to 3:6)

"And the people of Israel did what was evil in the sight of the Lord and served the Baals; and they forsook the Lord, the God of their fathers, who had brought them out of the land of Egypt; they went after other gods" (2:11-12).

Because every locality had its own unique form of Canaanite deities, we find their names pluralized in such verses as 2:11,13. And the Israelites, living among the Canaanites, were influenced by the religious practices of their neighbors. They forgot the Lord, the God of the desert and of the conquest. They forgot the One who had delivered, guided, and given victory to the generations before them.

In these verses we see the first expression of the cycle that forms the literary backbone of this book: sin, punishment, repentance, and deliverance. Let's look at each of these four elements as summarized in this passage.

The sin is presented in verses 11-13. Evil-doing, forgetting and forsaking the one true God, and serving the Baals and the Ashtaroth provoked the Lord to anger.

Some call verse 14 the key verse in this passage. When the anger of the Lord was kindled against Israel, he gave them over to the power of their enemies who were all around them. They were no longer able to stand against their enemies. Whenever they marched into battle, the Lord's hand was against them instead of against their foes (vv. 14-15). These invasions and defeats were not historical accidents; they were the punishment of judgment. The Lord was doing exactly what he had warned he would do. And he brought his judgment through the ordinary processes of history, through invasion and oppression.

The next phase of the cycle, the phase of repentance and crying to the Lord for help, is implied in the passage. The goal of the judgment was clearly to make people aware of their sin and need so that they would turn back to the Lord. And verses such as 17 and 18 indicate that the people did return to the Lord for brief periods of time and that the Lord responded in mercy.

The Lord's forgiveness found historical expression in the appearances of the deliverers we call judges. These leaders saved the people in a physical and material sense. They saved them from the power of those who plundered and oppressed them (v. 16). We can also see in verse 18 that these judges were charismatic (Spirit-gifted) leaders. The Lord was with each of the judges. His favor rested on them. His Spirit gave special gifts to them.

Unfortunately, after a brief period of following their fathers' wholesome example, the people refused to listen to their judges and committed spiritual adultery with other gods all over again (2:17,19). Why does apostasy often seem so much more persistent than faithfulness?

At any rate, the Lord's anger was kindled against Israel again and again. The people had so consistently and clearly violated his covenant with them that God declined to drive out before them any of the nations that were left in the land when Joshua died. Rather, he would use them to test Israel. These pagan peoples would become a test of Israel's faith, an indication of how truly Israel would walk in the Lord's ways.

The first six verses of chapter 3 list the nations who dwelled among Israel (and vice versa). The five lords of the Philistines (v. 3) were five overlords who ruled the five Philistine cities. The Sidonians were the Phoenicians of the northern coast who took their name from their country's primary city, Sidon. The Hivites were Hurrians who penetrated down into the area outlined in verse 3 and left behind pockets of settlers.

One authority notes that verse 6 speaks of conquest by matrimony. The Canaanites accomplished in times of peace what they had failed to do by military means. Their children married the children of Israel, and both sides served the gods of Canaan.

The stage is set for the repeated story of apostasy, punishment, repentance, and deliverance. In other words, enter the judges.

During the Time of the Judges (3:7 to 16:31)

Six judges are no more than names and are disposed of in two or three verses. Others, like Deborah, Gideon, and Samson, are given two to four chapters. The enemies they faced were generally their near neighbors, and almost always those on the fringes of the land rather than the Canaanites who actually lived in it.

In defensive matters, the tribal league was evidently based on the NATO concept: When one tribe was attacked, all the other tribes would come to its aid. In actual practice, however, there was no central leadership to rally the forces during these recurring emergencies. At times the judge was a strong enough leader to rally at least the neighboring tribes to help blunt the invasion. But the judge himself was clearly the man of the moment, and the central figure in each account.

Othniel (3:7-11)

The first judge named was associated with the tribe of Judah. He was related to a strong leader, Caleb, even if he was not such a significant leader himself. Othniel was a kinsman of Caleb and his son-in-law, and thus was a member of the Kenizzite clan in the tribe of Judah (Josh. 15:13-19; Judg. 1:11-15).

The first element in the cycle was sin. The people lapsed into paganism. They did evil in the sight of the Lord. They forgot him, but they remembered the false gods, whose names are again in plural form. Asheroth is the plural of Asherah, Baal's female consort. It is used in its singular form to refer to the wooden pillar that symbolized the goddess at the local shrines.

Verse 8 describes the phase of judgment and punishment. This king and his kingdom are unknown to us except for this reference. He probably came from northern Mesopotamia, though some scholars locate his realm in nearer areas, and he dominated the Israelites for a relatively brief period of eight years.

The next verse tells that the people of Israel finally cried out to the Lord. When they thus repented and returned to him, he raised up someone to deliver them. The Spirit of the Lord came upon Othniel (3:10). The word translated "Spirit" can also mean "wind." The Spirit of the Lord came upon these judges in an almost wind-like way to equip them for unique activity. God's Spirit could convey physical strength, wisdom, or artistic skill. It could impart leadership qualities or the ability to persuade people. Othniel received a spirit of heroism, of courage, and military skills like those Joshua had before him.

This endowment of the Spirit was evidently temporary. This is in direct contrast to the role of the Holy Spirit in New Testament (and present) times. Rather, the Spirit came upon the judges in times of crisis and enabled them to meet the challenge of the day.

Notice that this paragraph ends with a round number, "forty years," a characteristic of Judges, and with the simple statement of the death of the judge.

Ehud (3:12-30)

The oppression by Eglon of Moab (3:12-14).—Same song, second verse. "The people of Israel again did what was evil in the sight of the Lord" (v.

12). And when they once again did evil, the Lord's judgment fell again.

When the Scripture says that the Lord strengthened Eglon, the king of Moab (v. 12), it is saying that the Lord was in control of the situation. He accomplished his purposes through a little nation that was strong during several of these centuries. Its king, Eglon, allied himself with desert tribes called Ammonites and Amalekites. This alliance successfully invaded Israelite territory. It captured Jericho, the city of palms. It may have been responsible for one of the destructions of Bethel. The resulting oppression lasted eighteen years.

Ehud's plot (3:15-25).—When the people of Israel finally began to cry to the Lord, he raised up Ehud, a member of the Gera clan of the tribe of Benjamin. He was left-handed, as were many of the soldiers of his tribe. He supervised the delivery of the tribute to Moab, which probably included oil, wine, animal skins, and wool.

Before he left on one particular mission, Ehud decided that enough was enough. He prepared a two-edged dagger, a foot to a foot and a half long, evidently without a cross guard. He concealed it by strapping it to his right thigh. No guard would think to look for it there, but it would be easily accessible. Ehud and those with him went through the normal tribute process. They even returned most of the way home. But at Gilgal he sent his associates on and turned back for a private meeting with Eglon. The "sculptured stones" and Seirah of verses 19 and 26 were landmarks well-known to them but unknown to us.

Ehud gained his audience with Eglon by claiming to have a secret message for him. "Cloak-and-dagger" is a modern expression, but the approach is ancient. Eglon silenced all his attendants and ordered them out of his presence. The two men were left alone in the cool single room built on the roof of the palace.

Ehud repeated his claim: "I have a message from God for you" (v. 20). At this news Eglon stood up, making himself more vulnerable to Ehud's attack. (Verse 17 has already informed the reader that "Eglon was a very fat man.") When Ehud struck Eglon with the dagger, it disappeared into his abdomen, hilt and all. The resulting intestinal discharge hastened his death. Ehud calmly closed and latched the room's double doors and escaped.

Eglon's unsuspecting servants went to check on their master. When they found the doors locked, they thought he was relieving himself. As time passed, they grew perplexed, then confounded, and then alarmed. When he still did not open the doors, they used a key to open them and found their king dead on the floor.

The defeat of Moab (3:26-30).—Ehud had escaped completely during the delay. When he reached the western side of the river he rallied the troops from the hill country of Ephraim. He promised them victory over their oppressors in the name of the Lord.

Ehud's first act during the battle was to seize the crossings of the Jordan River and cut off the retreat of the Moabite occupation troops. The enemy was caught completely off guard and annihilated in the slaughter that followed. Ten thousand Moabite soldiers fell, and Moab was subdued (v. 30), in the sense that the invasion forces were driven out. The land remained comparatively secure for some eighty years, two biblical generations. There is no indication that Ehud's leadership continued after this crisis was resolved. Like the other judges, he was a temporary leader who served for "the duration."

Shamgar (3:31)

Shamgar is the first minor judge, though this verse doesn't give him the title "judge" or locate him as to tribe. His name may be Hurrian, not Semitic.

Like Ehud, Shamgar used an unusual means to eliminate his enemies. An ox goad was a long wooden pole with a metal tip at one end and a metal blade on the other. It was used to clean the plowshare during the plowing. It was an unusual weapon, but an effective one.

Shamgar is mentioned in the Song of Deborah (5:6). His was a day of curtailment of caravan trade because of raids by enemies such as the Philistines. Shamgar is one of the many Bible characters we would like to know more about.

Deborah and Barak (4:1 to 5:31)

There are several reasons this extended record is important. This is the last account of opposition from the Canaanites. The rest of the book of Judges is concerned with invaders from the fringes of the country. The encounter was both crucial and decisive. It was the greatest military victory of the period. It involved the status of the Esdraelon Plain. As long as that area was under Canaanite control, it was a wedge cutting Israel almost in half.

This section is of further interest because it tells the same story twice, in prose in chapter 4 and in poetry in chapter 5. The Song of Deborah (chapter 5) is incomparable. Commentators exhaust their descriptive powers in pay-ing it tribute and do the same with regard to the heroine of the famous song. The record is popular and well worth studying.

Canaanite oppression (4:1-3).—Chapter 5, verse 8, may hint at the nature of the evil Israel did after Ehud's death (v. 1). They turned away from the Lord in the sense that they chose other gods. As they settled into an agricultural life, they felt more need of a god who promised to make the soil fertile than of a God who had proved to be a leader in the desert wanderings and a help in battle.

Once again the Lord sent his judgment within the processes of history. Jabin was a king in Canaan. He ruled from Hazor, just over eight miles north of the Sea of Galilee. At one time his city covered two hundred acres and was the most populous in Canaan. Our present story took place around 1125 BC, a century after Joshua conquered a king of the same name in the same area.

Jabin is not mentioned in the Judges 5 account. The prominent person there is Sisera, who served as a military leader for the Canaanite coalition. He lived in Harosheth-hagoiim, probably sixteen miles northwest of Megiddo on the Kishon River. The Iron Age had begun among the Canaanites but had not reached the children of Israel. Sisera commanded a large army of iron chariots. In other words, as Israel faced the Canaanite war machine, she was outnumbered and poorly equipped.

Of course, the northern tribes were the ones primarily affected by the Canaanite oppression, and especially those that bordered the Esdraelon Plain. The Israelite invaders had originally confined themselves to the hills, but they could not help being attracted by a rich plain like this one. It was a commercial lifeline, the main trade route from Egypt to Mesopotamia, and it was guarded by fortified Canaanite cities, such as Taanach and Megiddo.

The leadership of Deborah (4:4-9).—Deborah was a mighty woman of valor. She became the rallying center for Israel against the long-time oppression. Verse 4 calls her a prophetess and a judge. She had gifts of insight, foresight, and wisdom. She also was a part of the judicial processes of Israel. She served as an elder to dispense justice at the gate. People went to her for advice and for the settlement of their disputes. (She was a judge in our modern sense of that word.) All in all, people depended on her as a channel of guidance from the Lord.

It was in this capacity that Deborah sent for Barak. She summoned him to her, an indication of the considerable authority she exercised over him. She gave him detailed instructions from the Lord.

Barak was to gather his troops at Mount Tabor. These troops were to come from the tribes of Naphtali and Zebulun. Chapter 5 adds Ephraim, Manasseh (Machir), Benjamin, and Issachar. Mount Tabor was twelve miles from Megiddo at the northeast end of the Esdraelon Plain, a strategic center for the beginning of the campaign.

The build-up of such an army would attract Sisera's attention and prompt him to move to intercept it. But in order to meet the Israelites at their prominent location, he would have to cross the plain and the Kishon River. Although we call it a river or a brook, it was only a dry streambed in the summer. During the winter, however, it could become a raging torrent (5:21).

Deborah promised that the Lord would give Sisera into Barak's hand (v. 7). Barak accepted his responsibility as general, but with a significant reservation. He insisted that Deborah accompany him. She agreed; however, she responded that because of the weakness of his faith, he would not gain the glory in the victory. The glory for the triumph would go to a woman, and Deborah was not talking about herself.

The rout of the Canaanites (4:10-16).—Kedesh, where Barak mustered his ten thousand men, was located in the southern part of Naphtali, between Mount Tabor and the Jordan River, forty miles northeast of where the battle was later joined. When Sisera heard what was going on, he mobilized his forces for the attack.

We wish we had more details about the battle. A sudden rainstorm turned that plain into a muddy bog. Sisera's fearsome iron chariots were completely helpless. His men were easily defeated by the more mobile Israelite foot soldiers. The defeat was complete. The entire enemy army was slaughtered. "Not a man was left" (v. 16). As for Sisera, he had to flee from the battlefield on foot—in other words, in utter defeat.

The death of Sisera (4:17-24).—The exhausted Sisera found refuge in the tent of a supposed friend. Heber the Kenite had separated himself from the Kenite clan of Jobab and had migrated from the wilderness of Judah near Arad (1:16) northward to a location not far from the scene of the battle under consideration. Though they were a nomadic tribe, the Kenites had thrown their lot with Israel. Jabin's coalition had not oppressed the Kenites, so Sisera considered them to be friends (v. 17). He did not realize how closely they were aligned with Israel.

Jael, our other heroine, the wife of Heber, made the first move. She went out to meet Sisera, showed him kindnesses, and reassured him. She invited him into her tent and urged him not to be afraid. She provided a covering for him. She gave him milk to quench his thirst. Soon he fell asleep as she stood guard.

Among bedouins it was the woman's job to put up the tent. Jael was familiar with all the necessary equipment. As Sisera slept, this daughter of a ruthless, violent age took a tent stake and a hammer and pinned Sisera to the ground through his temple. When she left the tent a second time it was to summon Barak, hot on Sisera's trail, to see his dead enemy. The victory *had* been secured by a woman. With the tide turned against the Canaanites, the people of Israel were able to press on to eventually win a complete victory (vv. 23-24). They probably did not completely control the Esdraelon Plain after this engagement, but they did have free access through it.

The Song of Deborah (5:1-31).—Chapter 5 is the poetry version of the story. It follows the same general outline as chapter 4. Scholars are in much more agreement about its date and value than they are about the rest of the book of Judges.

This song was written in the twelfth century BC, about the time of the events described, and by an eyewitness, perhaps even Deborah herself. It is the most characteristic example of early Hebrew poetry. It has inherent literary power. It especially exhibits the rhythm and parallelism so characteristic of poetry in the Old Testament.

The song begins and ends with expressions of praise to the Lord. Fourteen times it describes him as Israel's God (see vv. 3,5). He is pictured as coming to his people's aid from his dwelling on Mount Sinai where he had shown himself to Moses and had established his covenant with his people (v. 5). Seir and Edom (v. 4) are two names for the same region (see Gen. 32:3; Deut. 33:2).

Verses 6-8 describe the situation in Israel before the appearance of Deborah. The people's unfaithfulness had resulted in such a lack of security that the normal activities of life ground to a standstill. Farming, travel, and trade became impossible. The highways were unsafe and therefore deserted. Travelers had to stay on the side roads to keep from being robbed. People had few weapons with which to defend themselves. Their well-armed opponents caused them to walk in fear.

Beginning in verse 9 praise is given for the tribes who participated in the campaign against the Canaanites and ridicule for those who did not. Six of the tribes from Benjamin north responded to the call to arms. Those less immediately affected were also less enthusiastic about going to war.

Deborah's tribe, Ephraim, is named first. Machir (v. 14) was the principal clan of Manasseh and evidently represented that tribe. Barak, the son of Abinoam (vv. 1,12), represented Naphtali. Zebulun and Naphtali are singled out for particular praise for risking their lives and their existence in the cause (v. 18).

Reuben, as usual, was indecisive (vv. 15-16), like an unresponsive sheep who heard but didn't leave the fold. Gad (Gilead in v. 17) also stayed away. During the time of the Judges, Dan relocated from the south, between Philistia and Judah, to the far north. Scholars differ as to which area the singer had in mind here. Both Dan and Asher are associated with maritime activities, perhaps in the sense of sea trade, perhaps through such neighbors as the Phoenicians, who were always seafaring people.

The battle scene in this chapter (vv. 19-22) is relatively brief. It makes up in graphic impact what it lacks in length. Taanach (v. 19) was four miles from its sister fortress, Megiddo. "The waters of Megiddo" were of course the Kishon River, which suddenly overflowed its banks and flooded the area.

The enemy's cause was hopeless from the first because of "the triumphs of the Lord" (v. 10). Israel so identified herself with the Lord that her enemies were his enemies and her victories his victories. He caused even nature to join in the battle against the Canaanites. The sudden storm was a sign of the Lord's presence to fight for his people (see nature's participation in vv. 4,20-21). The contrast here is not between the mighty kings of Canaan and the lowly Israelite infantrymen; the contrast is between those rulers and the Lord of the stars of heaven.

Meroz (v. 23) was a village near the Esdraelon Plain. It lay in the path of retreat for Sisera and his army. In verse 23, its people are bitterly cursed for not apprehending the enemy general as he escaped. Jael, of course, saved the day. Sisera expected hospitality and protection from her. Instead, she used her improvised weapons to deal him a fatal blow.

One of the most poignant passages in the Bible (vv. 28-30) imagines what it must have been like in Sisera's palace as his mother and her attendants awaited his return from battle. In the scene, she watched for him expectantly and impatiently, confidently and hopefully, yet with some fear. He should have returned already. Her maidens assured her that the reason for the delay was the longer time it took to divide the excessive spoil of battle. And so they waited.

The noted song ends (v. 31) with a twofold wish, both negative and positive. The poet asks that the same fate (as Sisera's) may befall all of the enemies of the Lord, and that, on the other hand, all his friends may rise like the sun to drive away the darkness and to bring light and blessing to the land.

Gideon (6:1 to 8:32)

Gideon was an important little man. This book gives more space to him than to anyone else, except Samson. He led his people both militarily and spiritually. He delivered them from a severe oppression. He won a smashing victory against overwhelming odds, though in the beginning he was a nobody. And throughout his life he showed dignity and bearing that impress us.

By this point in Judges, the writer has moved away from the idea of war with the native inhabitants of Canaan to descriptions of the necessity of protecting Israel's territorial gains from the invasions of outsiders. This is the pattern for the rest of the book.

The oppression by the Midianites (6:1-10).—First the sin—as always— and then the punishment. These Midianite oppressors were desert peoples from the south and east of Moab and Edom. They were distantly related to the Hebrews (Gen. 25:1-2). The Amalekites came from the southern desert below Judah. The "people of the East" were from across the Jordan to the east. Nomads like these moved about in search of summer pasture. They usually remained along the margin of the desert, but they also made incursions into cultivated areas. Some of these incursions carried them as far as the Philistine area of Gaza. The area around Shechem suffered the most.

One advantage the Midianites and other invaders had was the use of camels. This was a new challenge to Israel. This is the first Old Testament reference to camels since Isaac, and may well be the first historical reference to their use in warfare. The camels provided mobility. Camel bands could cross long distances for surprise attacks on settlements. The Israelites were in danger of losing everything they had gained through conquest.

During seven consecutive harvest seasons these desert raiders swept into fertile agricultural areas. Their tents and families came next, to make camps and swarm over the crops like locusts until the land lay waste. Then they would move on.

The Israelites were forced to flee to mountain strongholds, making their homes in dens and caves. Truly "the hand of Midian prevailed over Israel" (6:2). The people of Israel were brought very low. The wonder is that they did not cry to the Lord for help sooner.

The Lord's first response to his people's cries was to send a prophet to them. Except for Deborah, this is the only reference to a prophet in Joshua and Judges. This spokesman for the Lord reminded the people of the Lord's leadership when they were in bondage in Egypt. He reminded them of the God-given victories over their enemies and the gift of the land.

Verse 10 is the crux of the prophetic message: "I am the Lord your God; you shall not pay reverence to the gods of the Amorites." Of course, that was the whole problem. The people had not paid any attention. Notice that the prophet offered no hope. But can it be that this message started Gideon thinking?

The call of Gideon (6:11-24).—When the Lord began to look for a deliverer for his people, he didn't start in a very likely place. Gideon was hiding out like all the other Israelites, threshing wheat in an abandoned winepress. Threshing floors were generally on the tops of hills, to make use of the prevailing breezes. A winepress would be at the foot of a hill. And there was Gideon, beating out grain by hand. He knew that if he threshed his wheat openly, the rising dust cloud would attract the Midianite raiders.

It was there, somewhere near Shechem, that an angelic messenger assumed human form. Imagine Gideon's shock when his visitor told him that the Lord was with him, and called him a mighty man of valor (v. 12)! But Gideon was affected by the same defeatist attitude as his people. He took exception to the angel's assertion.

"If the Lord is with us," Gideon argued, "why have all these bad things happened to us? Is the Lord with a people who have suffered so much? Isn't all this suffering an indication that he has forsaken us? Where are all the miracles of our past, such as the deliverance from Egypt, if the Lord is still with us?" (author's paraphrase). Gideon's conclusion was that the Lord had cast them off and given them into the hand of Midian (v. 13).

The Lord's answer through his messenger was that Gideon was to go forth in his might and deliver Israel. And Gideon responded (in essence): "Who, me?" He continued to be skeptical and full of doubts. Like so many leaders called in the Bible, he began to offer excuses. Neither his family nor his personal background gave much promise of success. All he lacked were the strength, notoriety, and experience for the job.

"I will be with you" (v. 16) is the Lord's answer to all reservations. Even the "weakest" and "least" (see v. 15) plus the Lord equal certain victory. The truth is that this sense of personal inadequacy is one prerequisite for fitness for the Lord's service.

Gideon asked for a sign that he had found favor with the Lord. He asked permission to offer a present to the Lord through the messenger (vv. 17-18).

He prepared a meal and placed it on a rock. The angel touched it with the tip of his staff. Fire sprang from the rock and consumed the offering. Then the angel vanished (vv. 19-21).

It was only then that the full impact of what had happened hit Gideon. He had been in the presence of the Lord! His sense of unworthiness was mixed with actual fear for his life. The Lord reassured him with a message of peace. In response, Gideon built an altar there and called it "The Lord is peace" (v. 24). It was still standing when Judges was written.

Attacking the Baal cult (6:25-32).—Gideon's first step of deliverance may have been the most difficult of all, but reformation had to begin at home. Gideon felt the need to get his own house in order. There was no hope of delivering Israel from outside oppression unless there was first an attack on the pagan worship in the people's hearts. Gideon was thus one of the first leaders in Israel to attack Baal worship.

Gideon's father seems to have had a background in the worship of the Lord. His name means "the Lord has given." However, he had been greatly influenced by the paganism of his Canaanite environment. The Asherah were fertility trees or, more probably in this case, wooden poles set up at Canaanite sanctuaries. When the pagan site was devastated and the Lord's altar was built instead, one of the two bulls used to demolish the altar to Baal was offered as a burnt offering to the Lord.

You can see why Gideon worked at night (6:27) when you see the uproar his action caused among the men of the area. This shows how thoroughly the Canaanite outlook had infiltrated Israel. But Gideon's courage inspired his father to return to his previous devotion to the Lord. Anyway, as head of the family he would have been responsible for the actions of his son.

The mob wanted to kill Gideon, but Joash turned their pagan superstitions against them. He accused them of sacrilege worthy of death for wanting to fight Baal's battles for him. "Does Baal need *your* help? What an insult to a god! You are the ones who should die for insulting Baal! If Baal is really a god, let him take care of himself and destroy the one who broke apart his altar!" (v. 31, TLB). Since it was a battle between the gods, he argued, they should be left alone to fight it out. Baal ought to be able to look out for himself.

From then on Gideon was also known as Jerubbaal. The new name means "Let Baal contend against him." The very fact that Gideon was still alive after attacking the pagan altar seriously weakened the case of the Baal worshipers.

The signs of the fleece (6:33-40).—Not long afterwards, the Midianites and the other desert clans made one of their yearly invasions. They crossed the Jordan and encamped in the Jezreel Valley at the eastern end of the Esdraelon Plain. This is one of the most fruitful areas in Palestine, and also open to invasions from the east.

In verse 34 another emphasis is made on the Spirit of the Lord. The Hebrew literally says that the Spirit of the Lord put on Gideon like a garment. Gideon was possessed by a power beyond himself. He sounded the trumpet to call out an army. His people of Manasseh lived just south of the Jezreel Valley. Zebulun, Naphtali, and Asher lived to the north of it.

But Gideon still had doubts. He sought another visible, outward sign. People of his day placed great importance on such material tests. He left this experience confident of the Lord's presence and leadership. Here is a man who was growing steadily in personal character, in spiritual maturity, and in his ability to lead.

In the first instance the fleece of wool on the threshing floor was wet, but the ground around was dry. Perhaps Gideon felt that the fleece could have collected dew in a natural way, so he reversed his request. Again the Lord responded. Gideon was satisfied that the battle—and the victory—was at hand.

Preparation for the battle (7:1-15).—It was time to get ready for the actual attack. Gideon led his 32,000 men (v. 3) to a camp beside the spring of Harod at the foot of Mount Gilboa. The Midianites were about four miles to the north, on the other side of the Jezreel Valley. They were by the hill of Moreh in Issachar.

Then came the greatest shock Gideon had received since the Lord had chosen him in the first place: The Lord told him his army was too large. A strong Israelite army might feel that it had won the victory in its own strength. The Lord was the true leader of the army and the one who gave the victory. If the Israelite army were too powerful, this would detract from the Lord's glory.

The first elimination test was simple: Anyone who wanted to could go back home (see Deut. 20:8). The fearful, the hesitant, and the uncertain were dismissed. Twenty-two thousand of Gideon's 32,000 men left.

Since the Midianites numbered in the scores of thousands (see v. 12; 8:10), Gideon must have suffered another shock when the Lord told him the army was still too large. This time the men were led to a stream and observed as they drank. The final army was chosen not on the basis of physical strength, mental sharpness, or military experience, but on the basis of how they drank water.

Most of the soldiers dropped to their knees and drank directly from the stream. A precious few cupped their hands, dipped up some water and drank. These remained standing, ready for any emergency. So the water test eliminated the lazy and uncommitted in favor of the alert and watchful, who numbered three hundred.

In verse 7 we have the Lord's timely assurance to Gideon: "With the three hundred men that lapped I will deliver you, and give the Midianites into your hand." The rest of the soldiers returned home. This was comparable to the strategy of taking Jericho by simply marching around it.

That same night the Lord gave Gideon the orders to move out. But apparently he sensed that Gideon, as usual, had doubts. He allowed him to take his servant and slip down to the enemy camp. What he heard there constituted a final sign of the Lord's leadership and presence.

Gideon and his servant crept down into earshot of the outer Midianite sentries. One of these guards was telling another of a dream he had had. A cake of barley bread had tumbled into the Midianite camp and flattened a tent. His superstitious buddy gave the dream a gloomy interpretation. The tent represented the nomadic Midianite hordes. The cake of barley bread represented the Israelite farmer-turned-soldier, Gideon.

Was the soldier who interpreted the dream serious or joking? Were the Midianites that uncertain and demoralized, like the Canaanites Joshua had faced? Regardless, Gideon was immensely reassured. He went back to camp with the sort of story any commander would be glad to report to his troops on the eve of battle. The victory was as good as theirs.

The rout of the Midianites (7:16 to 8:3).—Gideon divided his handful of men into three companies of one hundred each. He gave each a trumpet, an empty clay pot, and a torch. The clay pot hid the burning torch. He instructed them to watch him and follow his lead at every point. At his signal they were to sound their trumpets and shout their cry of triumph (vv. 17-18).

The Hebrews divided the night into three watches of four hours each. Gideon had his men in place at the beginning of the middle watch, an hour or two before midnight, when the guard had just been changed.

Gideon's three hundred men took positions on three sides of the enemy camp, simulating an attack from three sides at once. The key element was, of course, surprise. The Israelites depended on the fearfulness of the enemy rather than on their own military force. They used the sudden loud noises and blazing lights to throw the Midianites into panic. In the darkness the nomads couldn't tell friend from foe. They probably thought there was a regiment of Israelites behind each trumpet and torch.

The Midianites began to attack each other. They fled in utter confusion. They rushed eastward into the Jordan Valley in order to cross the river and return to the highlands to the east. Zererah was in the territory of Ephraim. Abel-meholah was somewhere in the highlands of Gilead east of the Jordan. Tabbath was also in Transjordan, between Mabesh-gilead and Succoth.

As verse 24 says, Gideon issued a second summons (see 6:35). Three hundred men were enough to turn the tide of battle, but not enough to adequately rout the fleeing enemy. This time Ephraim joined the four other tribes. They took control of the crossings of the Jordan in order to intercept the enemy and cut off his retreat. In the process they were able to capture and kill two prominent Midianite leaders, Oreb and Zeeb.

During a lull at some time during the pursuit, the Ephramites expressed to Gideon extreme displeasure at being left out of so much of the fighting (v. 1). Ephraim had long been a prominent tribe in the north. It had played a key role in the original invasion of the land. It had a strategic location, and the central shrine of Shiloh lay within its territory. The Ephraimites felt slighted at being summoned so late in the process of deliverance. (Maybe they most resented missing out on the spoils of battle.)

Gideon showed yet another aspect of his greatness as a leader as he pacified this tribe which was so jealous of its position. He minimized his own efforts and magnified theirs. He pointed out that they had had the glory of capturing the Midianite leaders. The Lord had allowed them to do what counted most. They had thus retained their dignity.

The proverb in verse 2 indicates that the worst of Ephraim was better than the best of Manasseh. More literally it suggests that the leftovers of Ephraim were better than the choicest of Abiezer, Gideon's clan of the tribe of Manasseh. By quoting or perhaps even originating this proverb, Gideon depreciated himself and flattered and pacified the Ephraimites.

Pursuit beyond the Jordan (8:4-21).—The story takes up again with Gideon's pursuit of the fleeing Midianites. He and the three hundred had extended themselves considerably and expected help from their brothers on the eastern side of the Jordan. However, the men of Succoth and Penuel, two cities on the Jabbok River (see Gen. 33:17; 32:30-31), refused to supply the provisions requested.

The officials of these cities showed disdain toward Gideon. They rejected his leadership. They were unimpressed by all the Lord had done through him. We do know that the tribes on the eastern side of the Jordan had shown indifference before to their brothers on the western side (5:17). And perhaps they were skeptical of Gideon's prospects for success. They may have assumed that the Midianites would melt away into the desert to regroup and that Gideon's small band would be unable to seriously weaken them. They may have been afraid that they, so near the desert areas, would become victims of a later retaliation.

Gideon promised to return to punish the leaders of Succoth and Penuel after his victory and continued his pursuit. The Midianites probably felt that because they had made it back across the Jordan they were beyond the reach of their pursuers. They were at home in the desert, whereas the small army of peasants was not. They seriously underestimated the persistence of their Joshua-like opponent. Gideon caught up with them at Karkor, east of the Dead Sea. They were so confident that they had not even posted lookouts. Gideon once again caught them off guard, threw them into panic, and captured their kings (vv. 11-12).

The names of the desert leaders in this passage are different from those of chapter 7. Nomadic tribes have always been loose in organization. There were doubtless several tribal leaders as a part of the desert coalition that annually invaded Israel.

Gideon returned from this final engagement by a route we are unable to pinpoint. His immediate intention was to discipline the cities that, like Meroz (5:23), were cursed because they did not move to help the Lord's army. As he neared Succoth he captured a young man from the town. This fellow wrote down for Gideon the names of the seventy-seven city officials and family heads. Gideon threw the taunts of these city leaders back in their faces. He had fully done what they had ridiculed him for not having done (vv. 6,15). He exhibited the enemy leaders he had captured.

Most commentators think that Gideon tortured to death the disdainful city leaders. He taught (or threshed) the men of the city. He may have dragged them over thorns, as a threshing sledge is dragged over grain. At Penuel he wrecked the tower, the fortress of a town that may have lacked protective walls, and killed the men of the city.

The next paragraph in this chapter is equally brutal. It reveals a part of Gideon's motive in his relentless pursuit of Zebah and Zalmunna. They had killed his brothers at Tabor. He felt an obligation to seek blood revenge. The enemy leaders even admitted that the man they had killed had a royal bearing and the same general appearance as Gideon himself (v. 18). He said that he wanted to spare their lives but could not, in light of their deed.

Gideon offered to his oldest son Jether the right to kill the enemy rulers. This would have been a considerable honor to the boy and a considerable dishonor to them. But the young man hesitated. He didn't have the heart to carry out the command. The two rulers insisted, rather, that Gideon perform the deed. They would prefer to be killed by a hero rather than a youth.

It is difficult for us with our background of the teachings of Christ to understand such savagery. We must keep in mind that the standards of morality of that ancient day, even among the Lord's people, were much lower than ours, and that their understanding of the Lord and his will was still far from perfect.

Gideon's latter days (8:22-32).—Gideon's success was a sure indication that the Lord was with him. He was an obvious recipient of the Lord's Spirit and was clearly the most capable man in all Israel. The danger from the outside seemed over for a while, but since the land had been invaded by foreigners before, it might be again. Many people felt the need for a more efficient national organization and for more consistent, capable leadership.

Some of the Israelites began to think of Gideon in terms of kingship. A king would unify the various tribes, and Gideon had more than adequately demonstrated his suitability for leadership. This was the first attempt in Israel's history to establish a hereditary monarchy.

Gideon refused the offer. He insisted that Israel continue the theocracy with the Lord as direct ruler. We do know that there was always in Israel an ambivalent attitude toward the monarchy. In these early days, and much later, some felt that to want a king was to reject the Lord.

Gideon responded to the people's request with a request of his own. He asked for all the golden earrings among the spoil. Nomads like the Midianites (here called Ishmaelites) always carried their wealth with them. The treasure that Gideon received weighed anywhere between thirty-five and seventy pounds, depending on the scale used, in addition to other valuable items such as the ornaments on the necks of the camels (v. 26).

Gideon took the treasure and made an ephod, which he set up in his home city of Ophrah. *Ephod* has several different meanings in the Old Testament. Here it probably means "image" or "idol," or possibly some sort of priestly vestment so decorated with gold that it stood alone. The sad thing about Gideon's latter days is that "Israel played the harlot" (v. 27) after his ephod. The people engaged in idolatrous worship of this religious object. That is the bad news. The good news is that Midian had been completely and permanently subdued (v. 28).

Gideon lived to a ripe old age. He had refused the kingship, but he lived very much like an Oriental monarch. He had many wives and concubines, and fathered numerous sons. Of course, polygamy and concubinage were common in that day. Abimelech, whose mother may have been a Canaanite, is especially noted in verse 31. Through the infamous ephod and through this illegitimate son, the seeds of future trouble had already been sown.

Abimelech (8:33 to 9:57)

Abimelech was not one of the judges, but his is a fascinating story about an important character. Some people call this the most instructive story in Judges. It illustrates the undesirable aspects of the monarchy as it shows a trend in that direction.

This story also reaffirms our understanding that many Canaanites still lived in the land. Not only had they not been wiped out, they had retained control of several of the larger cities. This story tells how one such city came under Israelite control. It also shows a fusing of the Hebrew invaders and the original inhabitants of the land.

The repeated apostasy (8:33-35).—As soon as Gideon died, the cycle of apostasy resumed. Baal-berith means "Lord of a covenant." Chapter 9, verse 4 lists him as the local Canaanite deity at Shechem. Once again the Israelites forgot the true God who had done so much for them. They also forgot their debt to Gideon. They failed to show any gratitude or kindness to his family. Such a disturbed and godless time was ripe for the appearance of an ambitious and ruthless tyrant.

Abimelech's rise to power (9:1-6).—Shechem lay in the territory of Ephraim between the sister mountains of Ebal and Gerizim. The pass where it was located joined the coastal plain along the Mediterranean with the Jordan Valley. It had long been an important city in Canaan and may well have entered Israel's tribal confederation by treaty, not by conquest.

Abimelech was the son of Gideon, but his mother was a Canaanite. In the case of such a concubine, the mother retained custody of the child. She remained with her own clan, and was visited occasionally by her husband. Ophrah, Gideon's family home, was thirty miles to the north. Abimelech may have also lived there for a time when he came of age, before deciding that he could make his way to the top more quickly at Shechem.

Abimelech persuaded his mother's people to bend the ears of the people of Shechem for him. With Gideon, the unofficial ruler, gone, Abimelech suggested that it would be better for one to rule than many, and better a relative.

The people of Shechem showed that blood is thicker than reason and fell in with his plans. His mother's people were evidently people of influence, so much so that they even secured modest financing for Abimelech's "campaign" from the temple treasury (v. 4). Abimelech used this money to hire several "worthless . . . fellows" (v. 4, *RSV*) to assassinate his brothers. Only the youngest, Jotham, escaped. Then Abimelech was made king.

Jotham's fable (9:7-21).—It was during this coronation ceremony under the sacred oak tree that Jotham recited his famous fable about the trees. He was on top of Mount Gerizim, some seven hundred feet above the valley below, speaking into a natural amphitheater with excellent acoustics. He began with a summons of an almost judicial character. Everything he said seethed with irony and outraged justice.

In the fable, the trees wanted to select a king. They first approached their most worthy representatives. Each one refused. The olive was the most important fruit tree, but it preferred providing its oil to anoint guests, kings, and religious leaders and to be part of feasts and sacrifices. The fig wanted to continue providing its sweet food and the vine its drink and drink offerings.

Finally the trees approached, of all things, the useless and unworthy bramble. Imagine trees standing in the shade of a bramble. But the bramble accepted their offer, and accepted with demands and threats. It implied that it could harbor fire that could destroy even the majestic cedars of Lebanon (v. 15).

Jotham followed his fable with an interpretation. Gideon was obviously represented by the three fruit trees. He had rejected the kingship. The murderous Abimelech was no more than a bramble, without the wisdom or the ability to lead. He was not a man of integrity. He was not someone the people could put their confidence in. He could be of no help to the people, but much danger. Shechem would soon regret any support they gave him.

Jotham reminded the Shechemites of his father's gallantry on their behalf, and of how they had repaid his family with assassination (vv. 17-18). Notice the repeated "if's" in verses 16-20. He sarcastically suggested that his hearers would reap just as much "good faith," "honor," and "rejoicing" as they deserved. His parting shot, before he escaped, was to predict that fire would devour those who followed his half-brother (v. 20).

Rebellion against tyranny (9:22-41).—But Abimelech was king. He was king *in* Israel if not king *of* Israel. This chapter lists four cities under his control (vv. 6,41,50). His reign lasted all of three years. Then the Lord instituted the process that punished him and brought him down.

When we read verse 23 we need to remember that the early Hebrews tended to ignore indirect or secondary causes. They attributed everything, good or bad, directly to the Lord. In this case, the evil spirit was the Lord's judgment on Abimelech for his treachery. The result was that the men of Shechem began to deal treacherously with him.

As time passed, disloyalty and discord grew. Shechem's leaders began to ambush caravans that passed through their valley. This made normal commercial life uncertain. It may even have been a more direct attack on Abimelech's authority and income. Perhaps he had guaranteed safe passage to traders, charging them for protection.

Gaal may have been a Canaanite; he was certainly an opportunist. He moved into Shechem and gained the confidence of the leaders of the city. Then he bided his time until he could move openly. Perhaps this passage indicates that many of Abimelech's opponents gradually began to gather in Shechem.

Gaal's more formal revolt broke out at the end of a grape harvest. It gave him a chance to talk with a large group of people. Such festivals were exuberant and probably often boisterous. Gaal's words were the spark for the explosion that sealed the doom of King Abimelech and all those who had supported him.

Gaal picked up on all the normal complaining about "the government." (Abimelech was living in Armah and ruling through his governor Zebul, according to vv. 30,41.) He openly challenged Abimelech's authority and implied that he should be the ruler instead. Shechem was a strong, ancient, honorable, and important city, and it was being ruled by an interloper. Gaal genuinely tweaked the lion's nose (vv. 28-29). You can almost hear his cadences beginning with, "And if I am elected . . . "

Governor Zebul notified Abimelech that Gaal was stirring up the city and also suggested a plan of action. Abimelech should surround the rebellious city at night and launch a surprise attack at dawn (vv. 30-33). From then on everything went right for one side and wrong for the other. When Gaal saw the ambushers, Zebul ridiculed him and said Gaal was seeing the shadow of the mountains, not Abimelech's four companies of soldiers. Zebul clinched his taunts with the question, "Where is your mouth now?" (v. 38). Zebul goaded Gaal into going out to face Abimelech, whom he had ridiculed and despised. Many were wounded at the entrance of the city, and Gaal and his relatives were driven away.

The destruction of Shechem (9:42-49).—After taking care of his rival,

Abimelech reorganized to turn on the Shechemites. When the workers left the city to go to the fields, two of Abimelech's three companies attacked the workers while the third stormed the gate of the city. The inhabitants of Shechem were destroyed. The buildings were leveled. The destruction was total, as evidenced by the strange expression in verse 45. Sowing the city with salt was a way of wishing permanent desolation for it.

In Shechem the tower seems to have stood apart from the city proper. It was a special stronghold associated with the temple. It became the last refuge for many of the citizens. Abimelech gathered enough brush to set a raging fire around this tower, and destroyed a large number in a horrible fashion. Jotham's prediction had been literally fulfilled (see vv. 15,20).

The death of Abimelech (9:50-57).—Like so many others in the book of Judges, Abimelech met his end in an unusual way. Thebez, twelve miles to the northeast, had evidently participated in Shechem's revolt, so the vengeful ruler turned in that direction. He apparently took the city with ease. Once again, however, the people took refuge in a fortified stronghold. Abimelech was at the point of burning this tower as he had the one in Shechem when he became careless. He moved in too close to the tower wall. A woman dropped a millstone on his head and crushed his skull. He was conscious long enough to insist that his armor-bearer kill him so that he would not die at the hand of a woman.

With Abimelech dead, his army dispersed. His "kingdom" was no more. In this the Lord repaid him for his crime against his brothers and made the wickedness of Shechem fall back on its own head. Jotham's curse had come true, and the first Israelite effort at kingship had proved sadly premature.

Tola (10:1-2)

There are six minor judges in this book. Tola and Jair (vv. 3-5) are the second and third. These men receive only the barest mention. They are not associated with any specific enemy. We learn here only of their ancestry, home, and the length of their leadership. They were evidently tribal or regional leaders whose major role was the administration of justice.

Tola is associated with the tribe of Issachar and named as the head of a clan (Gen. 46:13; Num. 26:23). "Dodo" is a name that may indicate a chief. Shamir may refer to Samaria.

Tola led a northern Israelite alliance for twenty-three years. We surmise this from the fact that the center of his activity was in the hill country of Ephraim, not in his own tribe of Issachar.

Jair (10:3-5)

Jair served east of the area administered by Tola. He is associated with the tribe of Manasseh and the conquest of Gilead (Num. 32:41; Deut. 3:14). On the other hand, verse 3 calls him a Gileadite. Gilead was the highland area east of the Jordan.

Jair was a man of substance. This brief note indicates both affluence and polygamy. Each of his thirty sons was probably an aristocrat and the ruler of a city in the confederation called Havvoth-jair, the villages of Jair, whose center lay some ten to fifteen miles southeast of the southern end of the Sea of Galilee. Perhaps Jair was overlord of these several cities, each of which maintained its own government, as Shechem had under Abimelech.

Jephthah (10:6 to 12:7)

The story of this ill-fated deliverer illustrates how the tribal league worked, or rather did not work. In theory, when one tribe was threatened, the others would come to its aid. This rarely occurred, as we are about to see.

Renewed oppression (10:6-16).—We are used to introductory formulas like this one, but in this instance it is considerably longer. Verse 6 is a broad statement describing the political situation in western Palestine from the standpoint of its religious implications. The list of nations indicate peoples the Israelites had difficulty with at one time or another.

The Philistines may well have been mentioned in these verses to introduce the Samson stories in later chapters. The Samson stories lack an expected introductory statement. But the oppressors of the moment were the Ammonites. They were Semitic peoples who lived on the border of the Syrian Desert in central Transjordan. Their capital was Rabbah, the modern city of Amman, Jordan, twenty-three miles east of the Jordan River across from Jericho.

Gilead was East Manasseh. It bore the brunt of the initial Ammonite invasion (v. 8). Then the oppressors pushed westward across the Jordan into the central highlands to involve the tribes of Judah, Benjamin, and Ephraim.

Naturally, "the people of Israel cried to the Lord" (v. 10). In fact, we have here a paragraph of dialogue between the Lord and Israel. Israel confessed her sin of having forsaken the Lord for the Baals. However, the Lord responded by reminding her of how many times he had delivered her in the past only to have her lapse again into the worship of false gods. She had showed consistent ingratitude and evaporating obedience.

The Lord indicated that he was tired of having Israel go her own way until disaster struck and then feel a temporary need for the Lord. She had promised obedience so many times before but had never followed through that he declared, "I will deliver you no more" (v. 13). He mockingly challenged her to seek help from the heathen gods she had so repeatedly chosen.

Note the list of nations mentioned in verses 11-12. The Egyptians oppressed Israel before the Exodus. The Amorites were the original inhabitants of the area east of Jordan. The Ammonites were the present enemy. The Philistines invaded later in the time of Samson. The Sidonians may have been northern Canaanites such as Deborah resisted, or the term may indicate Phoenicians. There is no record of any Phoenician oppression of Israel.

The Amalekites were associated with Eglon of Moab (3:13) and with the Midianites Gideon conquered (6:3,33). The Maonites were an Arab group living east of Edom. They afflicted Israel in the times of Jehoshaphat and Uzziah (2 Chron. 20:1; 26:7). The early Greek translation of this verse reads "Midianites."

The people admitted their guilt as charged and continued to call on the Lord for deliverance. They turned away from the foreign gods, returned to the Lord, and threw themselves on his mercy. Typically, God was touched (vv. 15-16).

Selection of a new leader (10:17 to 11:11).—The danger to Gilead from the Ammonites was severe, especially when they gathered for an apparent direct attack. The people of the threatened area mustered at Mizpah, a religious center in north Gilead which has not yet been located. These people faced the dual problems of a strong enemy and the lack of a leader. So great was their need that they began to think in terms of making whoever would lead them their permanent head (vv. 17-18).

Enter Jephthah. He was a native son of Gilead and a courageous and effective fighter, but an outcast because he was illegitimate. His mother was not a lawful wife or even a concubine like Abimelech's mother. He had no hereditary rights. Rather, he was excluded from any family relationship, as if his situation were his own fault. He became the leader of a band of outlaws in the area of Tob, fifteen miles east of Ramoth-gilead (vv. 1-3).

As the war clouds continued to darken, the elders of Gilead finally approached Jephthah and invited him to be their leader in the fight against the Ammonites. He was brutally frank with them. He asked about the sudden change of attitude toward him. Apparently some of the qualities that forced him outside the law in time of peace they considered valuable in time of war.

Jephthah agreed to help the people of Gilead out of their immediate distress if he could remain as their leader after the war (vv. 8-9). The elders had little choice. The two parties entered into some sort of covenant. Each side agreed to the conditions stated. Moreover, the Lord was considered a witness (literally, "hearer") of all of the proceedings (v. 10).

Unsuccessful diplomacy (11:12-28).—Jephthah began immediately to act as king. He wanted to avoid outright war if possible. He sent a diplomatic mission to the king of the Ammonites to determine that ruler's reason for threatening war. During this period the Ammonites had begun to profit greatly from the development of caravan trade. They wanted to expand those interests into the Israelite portions of Transjordan. In fact, they wanted all of Israel's territory in Transjordan for themselves.

What the Ammonite king called "my land" in verse 13 was the kingdom of Sihon the Amorite. It had extended from the Arnon to the Jabbok Rivers. Jephthah went to considerable lengths to disagree with his opponent and effectively state Israel's claim to this territory occupied by the tribes of Reuben and Gad. As he did, he had to mention also the kingdoms of Moab and Edom.

Sihon's territory had originally belonged to Moab. When Israel appeared on the scene, she took no land from either Moab or Ammon (v. 15). She respected their rights. Israel requested permission to travel through the territories of Moab and Edom. They refused; Israel accepted their decision without question and, instead of trespassing, respectfully made a detour (vv. 17-18).

Israel also asked permission to pass through Sihon's territory. He not only refused, he attacked. Israel defeated him and annexed his territory. Thus Israel held Sihon's former kingdom by right of conquest (vv. 19-22).

Jephthah gave the Lord credit for dispossessing the Amorites and giving Israel the land. He challenged Ammon to depend on its god, as Israel had on hers. Chemosh (v. 24) was the name of the god of Moab, but it may be that Ammon worshiped the same deity by another name.

Jephthah spoke of Chemosh as if he actually existed. Some people believe he thought of the Lord as existing alongside the gods of other nations. We do know that the people of his time and area thought of the various gods in that way in relation to their national territories. However, other scholars insist that Jephthah was merely being diplomatic in his phrasing.

The judge's next line of argument was historical, as his first had been. King Balak of Moab had been a contemporary of Sihon. His territory had been next door. Yet he never questioned Israel's annexation and never declared war against Israel. The Ammonites had a much less valid claim than Balak did. Even more, the Ammonites themselves had never raised a question about the territorial situation, not in all the centuries that had passed (vv. 25-26).

Heshbon was fifteen miles east of the mouth of the Jordan. Areor was twelve miles up the Arnon on the famous King's Highway that ran north and south through the desert. It had been over three hundred years since Israel had conquered Sihon. The three centuries apparently refer to the time span of the book of Judges.

The defeat of the Ammonites (11:29-33).—The king of Moab paid no attention to Jephthah's overtures. Thus, when the Spirit of the Lord empowered this already powerful warrior, he stirred up the men of both West and East Manasseh (Gilead) for war. They gathered at the shrine at Mizpah and moved to the attack along a line we are unable to trace. The slaughter was great and the victory complete. Ammonite power was broken for the next several decades.

This paragraph describes the beginning of one of the Old Testament's most pathetic and tragic stories. Before launching his attack, Jephthah made a vow to the Lord. He pledged that if the Lord would give the Ammonites into his hand, he would offer as a burnt offering whoever first came forth to meet him when he returned home in victory.

Many commentators think that Jephthah had a human sacrifice in mind from the beginning. Some feel he was trying to ensure the Lord's help in the battle. Others stress his effort to bargain with the Lord or buy his support. Some call him half-pagan. Others see here a man who expected a great blessing from the Lord and felt compelled to promise a great personal sacrifice in return. In any case, Jephthah was a man who misunderstood what it means to give the Lord our best.

The fulfillment of Jephthah's vow (11:34-40).—Women often left the house first to greet returning heroes (Ex. 15:20; 1 Sam. 18:6). The first one to greet the victorious Jephthah was his only child, a daughter. As soon as he saw her he tore his clothes in a traditional expression of grief. The glory of his military victory and his new position of tribal leadership had turned into despair. The account reminds us of a Greek tragedy.

This story underlines the importance of words among the Hebrews. Vows—in fact, words—were sacred. You did not have to make a vow, but if you did make one, you had to keep it. Jephthah's honor was very much at stake. Even his daughter recognized that he had to do what he had said he would.

It only makes the story more wrenching, but the daughter took two months with her attendants to lament over the fact that she would die unmarried and childless. Then the grisly act was consummated. The incident still moves us today, as it moved the entire nation (vv. 39-40).

Strife with Ephraim (12:1-7).—The men of Ephraim caused trouble for Jephthah, as they had for Gideon (8:1-8). They felt slighted again by not being included in the campaign against the Ammonites. Ephraim was the self-appointed leader of the tribes of the north and Transjordan and, true to form, they crossed the Jordan to take Jephthah to task at Zaphon, not far from the mouth of the Jabbok. They even threatened to burn down his house.

Jephthah made no attempt to appease the Ephraimites, as Gideon had done. He pointed out that he was the duly appointed leader in Gilead. Verse 2 may mean that the elders of Gilead had asked Ephraim for help before they called on Jephthah, or it may mean that Jephthah himself had summoned them to join him. If the latter was the case, they refused the invitation of the outlaw and outcast. Then his notable victory aroused their jealousy, and they were not able to share in the spoils of battle.

Jephthah gave a very practical reason for acting quickly, without delay. The immediate danger had demanded it. More importantly, the Lord evidently approved of what he had done, since he gave such a signal victory.

The statement in verse 4 seems to indicate that Ephraim and Manasseh were important tribes united by geography and long-standing tradition. They ridiculed the Gileadites, on the other hand, as migrants or fugitives from the two tribes. And though they were only a part of these major tribes, they had assumed authority to wage war. The statement implies a charge of arrogance or perhaps even sedition.

The Ephraimites were quick with their mouths, but Jephthah was quick to act. He decided that if they wanted to fight, he would be glad to accommodate them. The Gileadites fell on and quickly routed the Ephraimites. They cut off their retreat to their homes on the west bank by taking control of the crossings of the Jordan.

As the stragglers of Ephraim tried to get lost in the crowd and cross back to their homes, Jephthah's men put them to a simple test. They were asked to pronounce the term *Shibboleth,* which means either "a stream" or "an ear of grain." But there were dialectal differences within Israel. The

Ephraimites could not pronounce the "sh" sound. They said "s" instead. Because they spoke the wrong dialect and failed this pronounciation test, they proved themselves to be from Ephraim and were executed (vv. 5-6).

So Jephthah's story ended, as it had begun, with conflict. This fascinating man judged Israel for only a brief time (v. 7).

Ibzan (12:8-10)

Now we come to the last three minor judges. The name Ibzan occurs only here in all the Bible. He may have been from Judah, but more likely this Bethlehem was located in Zebulun (Josh. 19:15), ten miles north of Megiddo. He was a man of wealth and influence, as indicated by the size of his family. The marriages outside the group were designed to increase the clan's prestige and wealth. The family size also indicates the practice of polygamy and perhaps the beginnings of an almost royal court.

Elon (12:11-12)

Elon was also from Zebulun (Gen. 46:14; Num. 26:26). Aijalon was in central Palestine, perhaps near Rimmon.

Abdon (12:13-15)

Pirathon was located in Ephraim (1 Chron. 27:14), six miles west of Shechem. Again the size of the family indicates prominence and material well-being. In fact, maybe an upper class was already emerging in Israelite society.

The reference to the Amalekites is unusual (v. 15). They aided other groups in attacking central Palestine from their home in Transjordan (3:13; 6:3). Perhaps some of them settled in Ephraim.

Samson (13:1 to 16:31)

Samson is the last of the judges in this book, the most popular, and the strangest. There is more space given to his exploits than any other of the judges. His tribe was Dan. The neighboring Philistines were his enemy. It might be proper to say that fighting the Philistines made him. Samuel, Saul, and especially David also fought them.

The Philistines had been a seafaring people originally from Crete, the islands of the Aegean, and perhaps even mainland Greece. They migrated into the coastal area of Palestine during the late thirteenth and twelfth centuries. They affected and were affected by Canaanite culture. For instance, their god, Dagon, was the Canaanite grain god. But they brought with them the secret of smelting iron and thus introduced the Iron Age into Canaan. For decades they maintained a monopoly over the production of iron for farm implements and weapons.

The Philistines occupied the coastal strip in southwestern Palestine. There they built their walled cities, including the famous five independent cities. They frequently raided Israelite territory. Eventually they began to take over the valleys leading into the central highlands where most of the Israelites made their homes. They were a troublesome enemy until David's time.

Samson was the first Hebrew to stand up to them, but he was not a military leader like many of the other judges. He marshaled no concerted effort of any type and fought no pitched battles. He had no planned strategy. Rather, his life was a collection of helter-skelter individual adventures involving border clashes in an area measuring only three by seven miles.

For these reasons some commentators are negative in their evaluation of Samson. He has been called a swashbuckler, border ruffian, and wayward giant. He was dominant when he met the enemy, and he was vulnerable around women of questionable reputation. Yet he showed character traits that are appealing and even endearing. He was popular, and he was important because the Lord was with him.

The visit of the angel (13:1-7).—Verse 1 is the final statement of the cycle formula, here in abbreviated form. The significant things about it are that a new, powerful enemy appears, and that the period of oppression was unusually long.

The tribe of Dan was still in its original location in the south, between Judah and Philistia. Chapters 17—18 tell of Dan's migration to the north. Zorah was on the western edge of the hill country, fifteen miles from Jerusalem to the east and the major Philistine city of Ekron on the west. Manoah and his wife were a simple, godly, but childless couple.

Samson was a child of promise. His birth reminds us of that of Isaac. It was foretold by the angel of the Lord, who appeared to Manoah's wife. He was a messenger from the Lord, the kind so closely identified with the Lord in the Old Testament. She called him "a man of God" (v. 6) when she reported the incident to her husband. This expression is often used to describe a prophet or even someone superhuman. We see in this story a slowly developing realization of the nature of this special visitor.

The angel promised the woman a son and described him as a Nazirite, a man set apart to God. He differed from ordinary men in his abstinence from wine and strong drink, his refusal to cut his hair, and his avoidance of contact with dead bodies (Num. 6:1-21). Such a vow indicated special loyalty to the Lord and could last for a set period or for life. Samson's applied throughout his lifetime (v. 7).

Even the mother-to-be had to follow Nazirite standards of purity until the child's birth (v. 14). Wine was made from grape juice. Strong drink was made from other juices and from grain. Unclean foods included meat from animals considered unfit for food. The angel's special promise was that Samson would be the first Israelite to lead his people against the Philistines (v. 5).

As the woman reported the incident to her husband, it occurred to her that she had not had the presence of mind to ask the visitor who he was or where he was from. She was especially impressed with his appearance (v. 6).

Manoah's request and sacrifice (13:8-25).—Manoah responded to his wife's news with a noble prayer. He asked for a return visit so they would know what their responsibilities would be in training the child. He wanted to know what the boy's manner of life would be (v. 12). Again the angel appeared to the woman, this time in the field, but she soon summoned her husband. The angel repeated the instructions previously given (vv. 13-14).

Manoah wanted to honor his guest with a meal (see also 6:18-21 and Gen. 18:6-8). He was still thinking of the angel as a human messenger. The angel refused the hospitality and suggested that a burnt offering be prepared for the Lord (vv. 15-17).

This was when Manoah asked his visitor's name so he could properly honor him after the child's birth. In the Old Testament, asking someone's name had the impact of asking, Who are you? The angel so much as replied, "Why do you ask my name since it is beyond your power to comprehend it?" His name was beyond the human powers of understanding.

Manoah took the meat and grain and offered it on a rock. When the flame of the fire went up toward heaven, the angel ascended in the flame. The couple fell on their faces. They finally realized what had been taking place (v. 21). Manoah was afraid they would have to forfeit their lives because they had been in such close contact with the Lord. His wife wisely replied that since the Lord had gone to such pains to communicate his will to them and had also accepted their sacrifice, they would be spared (v. 23).

In this notable way Samson was born. His name means "little sun" or "sun's man." It was a common name in Canaan, but the Israelites often borrowed names from their neighbors.

The Lord was with Samson from the beginning. He blessed him with sound physical development and with general well-being. Mahaneh-dan (v.

25) means "camp of Dan," a temporary settlement not far from Samson's home. In places like that, the Spirit of the Lord began to come on him and stir him.

Samson's first infatuation (14:1-4).—We have no information on Samson's youth. The first story after his birth tells of his becoming infatuated with a Philistine girl. This account indicates what archaeological research reinforces. There was no open hostility at this time between the Israelites and the coastal invaders. There was rather a sort of uneasy, mutually suspicious accommodation, including travel, trade, and in unusual instances, intermarriage.

Timnah was a satellite of the larger city of Ekron. It was four miles down the slope, southwest of the camp of Dan. We can take this story to indicate how physically and culturally dominant the Philistines were over the Israelites.

Hebrew parents would normally choose a bride for their son and make the financial arrangements for securing her. The headstrong Samson made his own choice and asked his parents to cooperate. They protested and tried to talk him out of it. They used the standard term of reproach for the Philistines (v. 3). But Samson was stubborn and inflexible.

Verse 4 reminds us that in the early days the Hebrews saw everything that happened as ordered directly by God. The verse also reminds us that the Lord is able to use even a bad situation.

The wedding feast and the riddle (14:5-20).—The next scene shows Samson and his reluctant parents making the two-hour walk down to Timnah. Samson evidently made the trip several times, sometimes alone. During one of these trips he was threatened by a lion. He tore the beast in two with his bare hands. He was able to do so because of the empowering energy of the Spirit of the Lord. This is the first account of Samson's superhuman strength.

Samson did not tell anyone about his adventure (vv. 6,9). Verse 1 says that he had only seen the Philistine girl. When he was later able to talk with her (v. 7) she pleased him greatly, and enough time passed for the carcass of the lion to dry out and for bees to hive in it and produce enough honey for Samson and his parents.

Samson's wedding had several unusual features. There was no marriage price paid to the bride's father by the groom's father. The wife was to continue to live with her family, to be visited periodically by her husband. Only his parents were present from his own family. All his attendants, including his best man, were Philistines. The wedding was held in her home, not his. Apparently her parents were not any more enthusiastic about the arrangement than his were.

Some interpreters feel that Samson's father either refused to arrange for the marriage or was slow in doing so, so Samson took matters into his own hands. This may have also been true of the week-long wedding feast, a sort of stag party before the wedding. It was an Oriental custom on such occasions to entertain the guests with riddles.

The linen garments were quality undergarments. The festal garments were dress clothes for special occasions. Perhaps they were richly embroidered. The wager was so large that the Philistine men could not refuse, and neither side could afford to lose.

Samson's famous riddle had two parts and therefore two answers. It was based on his two experiences with the lion and its carcass (v. 14). He knew that no one could guess it because no one else knew about it. His opponents became concerned, then worried, then frantic. We can see here the tensions between the two peoples. Samson's attendants clearly feared humiliation.

On the fourth day the thirty companions threatened the bride. She would get the answer for them or they would burn down the house with her in it (v. 15). They knew the way to get to Samson, and so did she. She used the old "if you really love me you'll do so-and-so" approach.

Samson responded that his refusal to share the answer to his riddle had nothing to do with the measure of his love. He had not even told his parents about it (v. 16). But she kept on and eventually wore him down with her persistence. She wheedled the answer out of him as the thirty companions knew she would.

The companions must have been gleeful as they answered the riddle of the country bumpkin from Dan (v. 18). Samson was beside himself with rage (v. 19). Everyone involved knew what had happened. His proverbial assessment (v. 18) is a classic.

To pay off the huge gambling debt, Samson went twenty-two miles down to the major Philistine city of Askelon, killed thirty men, and stripped them of their festal garments. He left for home without consummating the marriage. His father-in-law interpreted his conduct to mean that Samson never intended to return. To save his daughter from the disgrace of rejection, he gave her to the best man.

The burning of the wheatfields (15:1-8).—Samson's anger eventually cooled, and he wanted to return to his wife. This happened at the beginning of June during a celebration connected with the wheat harvest. Samson took a kid as a gift, probably the customary present for such an occasion.

Imagine how the father felt when he had to break the news that the girl was married to the best man. He gave as his reason his impression that Samson hated her (v. 2). The father felt he had to come up with some way to placate this hot-tempered and wronged young man who had almost become his son-in-law. By offering Samson a younger and better looking daughter, the father admitted that he was wrong and Samson right.

Samson felt justified in the revenge he vowed to take. His response was to begin a sequence of bitter and brutal two-way retaliation. He caught three hundred foxes and tied them together in pairs, tail to tail. Between each pair of tails he placed a torch and lighted it. He turned the frantic animals loose in the fields of standing grain.

It may be that this destruction was a deliberate and persistent policy on Samson's part, over a period of several weeks in several different locations, rather than a single rash act. At any rate, the dry fields of mature grain burst into flames that destroyed all the crop and spread to the valuable olive orchards nearby (v. 5).

The Philistines responded in kind. They burned his wife and her father to death because Samson's involvement with them had precipitated the problem. Then it was Samson's turn to respond in kind. He swore revenge upon them, and swore not to rest ("quit," v. 7) until he accomplished it.

The slaughter was great. "Hip and thigh" (v. 8) is a proverbial expression indicating the magnitude of the slaughter. Finally Samson withdrew to the cleft of the rock of Etam, somewhere south of his home. The border between Dan and Judah was fluid, and Etam was evidently across the border in Judah.

Further encounters with the Philistines (15:9 to 16:3).—Samson had managed to cause an international incident, the sort that could explode into a problem of far-reaching significance. The Philistines pursued him into Judah to force his extradition. They threatened the people of Judah if they did not hand him over.

The people of Judah were secretly on Samson's side, but knew the danger of trying to protect him. He already had quite a reputation for strength, as evidenced by the large number mustered to secure his submission. They reminded Samson of the fact that they were dominated by their neighbors to the west, and he explained that the trouble all started when they caused him trouble (v. 11). Samson agreed to submit to the people of Judah on the condition that they make no attack on him themselves.

The place where all this happened was later called Lehi (jawbone) because of this incident. When the Philistines saw their tormentor bound with the two new ropes and delivered into their custody, they began to rejoice. But the Spirit of the Lord came mightily on Samson. He snapped the ropes as if they were burning strings and attacked the startled Philistines.

Samson's weapon was the fresh jawbone of an ass. Such a bone would be heavier and less fragile than a dry one. He killed many of the enemy and routed the rest. The number "thousand" is often used in Scripture as a round number indicating considerable size. Ramath-lehi (v. 17) means "the hill of the jawbone."

But even heroes have their weaknesses. After the battle Samson was so thirsty he felt he was about to die. He felt suddenly vulnerable to the Philistines (v. 18). The Lord answered his prayer for help by splitting a hollow stone so that water came out. The spring that so refreshed Samson was called En-hakkore, the spring of him who called (upon God).

Verse 20 reminds us that, though there is much to condemn in Samson's personal behavior, he did keep alive in Israel a spirit of patriotism during the long Philistine oppression.

The next to the last story of Samson's superhuman strength (vv. 1-3) is based on another of his amorous adventures. Those responsible for this book made no effort to play down his obvious moral weaknesses. We can see here that the people of that day connected the Spirit of the Lord more with physical strength and practical skills than with moral purity.

Gaza was thirty-six miles from Samson's home, the southernmost of the five major Philistine cities, on the edge of the Israelite hill country. While he was there he became involved with a prostitute. The authorities heard about his visit and set a trap for him. They surrounded the prostitute's house and posted an ambush at the city gate. They were ready to wait all night for Samson to come out if that proved necessary.

Perhaps, since the city gate was shut and barred, the Philistines relaxed during the night. They were confident that their quarry couldn't get away from them, and they planned to move in on him the next morning.

At midnight Samson got up and lifted the gate of the city out of its place. This included the panels, the side posts, and the bars. He shouldered the entire load and carried it forty miles to the ridge of central Palestine across from the city of Hebron. What about the guards at the city gate? Perhaps they were not on duty at that moment, or perhaps Samson acted right under their noses.

Samson and Delilah (16:4-22).—This climactic episode shows Samson's weaknesses rather than his strengths. He was a sucker for dangerous situations and willing women. He felt that the normal rules did not apply to him.

He had been involved in two disastrous incidents with Philistine women, but they were not enough to teach him his lesson. This third such encounter was the final, fatal one.

Sorek (v. 4) lay on the border between Dan and Philistia. It was a fertile area and had belonged to Dan before it had fallen to the Philistines. The eastern end of the valley of Sorek lay just below Samson's home at Zorah.

A few scholars think Delilah was an Israelite, because of her Semitic name and the location of her village. Even if she were, she was under Philistine influence. She was an insider with the rulers of the Philistines. She was alluring, self-seeking, and calculating. Samson probably visited her often. This gave her a perfect opportunity to accomplish the purposes of his enemies and collect for herself a considerable reward (v. 5).

Delilah asked Samson the secret of his strength. He deceived her three times. He told her that if he were bound with seven fresh bow strings he would become weak and like other men. These were gut cords made from animal intestines. Then he told her it would take seven new ropes that had never been used. Later he said that seven locks of his hair would have to be woven into a web of a loom and tightened with a pin. Notice that this third time he moved dangerously close to the truth.

Delilah suspected that Samson wasn't being truthful with her, but she had to try his suggestions in order to find out for sure. Each time, she sounded the alarm only to have him rise and escape, his power intact (vv. 9,12,14). It is fascinating that Samson never seemed to suspect her motives or lose confidence in her. She gently reproached him for his playful deceit (v. 10), and she persisted. She fretted, complained, and begged.

Finally she wore him out. She accused him of not really caring about her because he had mocked her and had not told her what she asked (v. 15; see 14:16-17). "She pressed him hard with her words day after day, and urged him" until "his soul was vexed to death" (v. 16). Finally he gave in and told her everything.

His hair had never been cut because of his Nazirite vow (see 13:5). She knew instinctively that he had finally told her the truth (v. 18). It is interesting that Samson had previously broken the other two parts of his vow. He had participated in the wedding feast where wine and strong drink were consumed (14:10), and he had often contacted dead bodies when he killed the Philistines.

When Samson slept again, perhaps in a drunken stupor, Delilah had someone shave off his hair. She tested him and could tell that his strength was truly gone (v. 19). When she sounded the fourth alarm he fully expected to rise up as before, but this time he was unable to respond to the crisis as he had on other occasions. Verse 20 is one of the most poignant in the Bible: "He did not know that the Lord had left him."

On this occasion the Philistines took no chances. They blinded Samson, bound him with bronze chains, and imprisoned him in Gaza (vv. 1-3). There in the prison he ground at the mill. The only bright note in an otherwise dismal section is the comment that his hair began to grow back again.

The end of Samson (16:23-31).—The god of the Philistines was Dagon (see 1 Sam. 5:1-7). He was the god of grain, not the fish god as earlier interpreters understood. The Philistines had many gods, but Dagon was the chief. He was the father of Baal. He had been worshiped in Mesopotamia as far back as the twenty-fifth century BC. The Philistines adopted him from the Canaanites.

The Philistines gave Dagon credit for delivering their archenemy into their hands. Whenever they saw Samson over the next period of time, they praised Dagon. They wanted to stage an appropriate celebration of thanksgiving (vv. 23-24). Apparently they didn't notice how Samson's hair was growing.

When the time for the feast came, Samson's captors became even more careless than he had been. As the wine began to take effect, someone had the bright idea of exhibiting Samson and adding to the evening's merriment at his expense (v. 25).

The architecture of the temple where they gathered was typical of the palaces and temples of Crete, where the Philistines originated. Twin pillars supported the major part of the roof. The more important celebrants gathered inside. Large numbers of others crowded upon the roof of the colonnade where they could see what was going on (v. 27).

Samson talked the boy who was leading him into taking him to the major support pillars. Then he made a pathetic prayer to the Lord. He prayed for one final display of strength, even if it meant forfeiting his own life. He expressed the idea that if he destroyed all of his enemies, such revenge would compensate for the loss of only one of his two eyes. He dislodged the pillars by pushing them off their pedestals. The roof, with its heavy weight of spectators, crashed down on the crowd inside. There was tremendous loss of life (v. 30).

This is not a very uplifting story. Samson was a weakling in every way that counted. The record of his profligate life is reported more for warning than for example.

Appendix
17:1 to 21:25

The final chapters of Judges do not deal with any judge or other leader of significance. In fact, only three persons are mentioned by name in these five chapters. The chapters deal rather with the experiences of two less important tribes, Dan and Benjamin, and they deal with internal matters rather than external circumstances such as enemy invasions.

These chapters graphically illustrate the lack of organization characteristic of the entire period of the judges. There was no central authority. There was competition between the tribes rather than cooperation. The situation was conducive to lawlessness, depravity, and spiritual decline.

Verses such as 17:6 lead us to believe that one purpose of these chapters was to demonstrate the need for a king. The individual tribes were unable to defeat the Philistines. The tribe of Dan suffered the humiliation of being forced out of its home area. Neither law and order nor religious purity could be maintained. In other words, as long as Israel remained a loose association of individual tribes, she was vulnerable. No wonder many people began to long for a king.

The Relocation of Dan (17:1 to 18:31)

Joshua 19:40-46 tells us that the Danites were originally assigned territory in southeastern Canaan, between Judah and Philistia. We know that later they were so well-established in the north that their location became proverbial: "From Dan to Beersheba" means from the extreme north to the extreme south. The Song of Deborah places them in the north (5:17), so they must have made their move quite early. Some people feel that they moved even before Samson's time; some think immediately afterwards. Those who hold the former view believe that the Danites mentioned in the Samson stories were pockets left behind after the migration described in these chapters. The latter position would be that Samson's recklessness worsened the tribe's situation.

Joshua 19:47-48 refers to the Danite migration, as does Judges 1:32. It is clear that pressure from their Amorite and especially Philistine neighbors caused the move. The Philistines took most of the tribe's original land and were a constant threat. There was a dramatic need for elbow room.

Micah's Image (17:1-6)

"The hill country of Ephraim" (v. 1) was a part of Palestine's central highlands, in this case north of Jerusalem. A man named Micah had stolen a considerable amount of silver from his mother. It may be that she had dedicated it to the Lord before it was stolen, making his deed all the worse. When he heard his mother curse the thief, he was moved to confess his crime.

His mother all too quickly overlooked the seriousness of what he had done. She could not take the curse back, but she balanced it with a blessing (v. 2). He restored the silver, and she set aside a part of it to make one or more religious objects.

There is disagreement about whether verse 3 refers to one or two images. A molten image was made from melted metal poured into a mold. A graven image was an idol carved from wood or stone. It may also mean an idol with a wooden core overlaid with some precious metal. The combination of the two terms may simply mean that a single molten image was involved. We seem to see two images in vv. 3-4 and 18:14,17-18 and one in 18:30-31. If there were two images, it may be that the Danites appropriated only one of them.

Verses 4-5 indicate that Micah had a household shrine, the kind of private place of worship where the father or someone he designated officiated. In this case Micah ordained one of his sons as the priest. The teraphim was a figurine. The ephod could have been a priestly garment, but in this case it seems to have been a small image.

Micah may have felt that he was worshiping the Lord through these objects, or perhaps he saw them as lesser local deities associated with his family or the agricultural area where he lived. Regardless, verse 6 blames this spiritual corruption on the fact that Israel did not have a monarch to keep the people in line.

Micah's Levitical Priest (17:7-13)

A young man with religious training appeared on the scene, looking for a bigger shrine to serve. In this case the term "Levite" seems to be a reference to a profession rather than to a tribe. This young man was a member of the tribe of Judah. We do know that remnants of the Levites were absorbed into the tribe of Judah during Israel's later history.

Micah either consciously or unconsciously wanted a *true* priest to give his modest little shrine prestige, and the Levite-for-hire wanted a more prominent position. They were quick to reach an agreement.

Micah called the young man "father" (v. 10). It was a title of honor. Micah made adequate financial arrangements with the young man and even treated him like a son. "The young man became his priest" (v. 12), and Micah thought that with a real Levite of his own he was guaranteed to have the Lord's blessings. He could not have been more wrong.

The Danite Spies (18:1-10)

Verse 1 is another reminder that Israel lacked a king to serve as a central authority and to guarantee law and order. It was this unsettled situation that allowed the tribe of Dan to act as it did.

Dan's position in its traditional territory in the south was steadily growing less secure. The Danites were crowded by Judah, Benjamin, Ephraim, the Amorites (1:34), and especially the Philistines (13:1; 14:4). Naturally they wanted land where they could be free from such oppression.

The Danites used an Israelite practice of long-standing: they sent out spies. These five men left to explore the possibilities of settlement farther north. Their first stop was at the home of Micah in the hill country of Ephraim.

While there, the spies became aware of Micah's Levitical priest. They recognized who he was because of his southern accent. They immediately tried to find out all about him. They learned from him the details of how he got there and what his functions were.

The spies didn't want to pass up the opportunity to use the services of this "man of God." They persuaded him to seek a word from God for them about the success of their mission. "Inquire of God" (v. 5) means to seek guidance for decisions and conduct. Perhaps this was done initially by casting sacred lots such as the Urim and Thummim. The Levite told them to go in peace and the assurance that the Lord would be with them and lead them.

Eventually the spies reached Laish, a hundred miles to the north. This city, called Leshem in Joshua 19:47, lay on the southern slope of Mount Hermon, at the source of one of the major headwaters of the Jordan. It was situated in a large, fertile area. Its residents were of Phoenician stock. They lived secure, prosperous, isolated lives. They were unprepared militarily and too far away to expect help from their Phoenician relatives (vv. 7,28). They would obviously be easy prey.

When the spies returned to Zorah and Eshtaol they included all this information in their report. They urged their fellow tribesmen to prompt action. They interpreted the situation as God-ordained (vv. 9-10).

The Migration of Dan (18:11-31)

Six hundred armed men, with families and belongings, set out for Laish. Some people interpret this number to mean the entire tribe did not migrate, but that pockets of Danites were left behind. More likely this was an advance migration, to secure the way for other, larger groups. This account may be called the concluding story of the conquest of Palestine.

The advance force made its first camp at Kiriath-jearim, one of the original towns in the Gibeonite league (Josh. 9:17). It lay six miles east of Dan's home region and eight miles northwest of Jerusalem. Then the group moved nearer the home of Micah.

At this point the spies suggested robbing the original robber, Micah. They told their brothers about the ephod, the teraphim, the image(s), and the Levite. So the armed men guarded the gate while the five spies stole Micah's image(s) and abducted his priest. Then they all continued northward.

The priest objected at first and was forcibly persuaded to cooperate. Soon, however, his alarm turned to joy. He was flattered by the considerable promotion. He would now serve as priest to an entire tribe rather than for one family. He accepted.

The Danites expected trouble from Micah. They placed their children, cattle, and possessions ahead of them so they could more easily defend the company from the rear. Eventually Micah caught up with them, he and a body of neighbors he had enlisted. He was angry, but the Danites were scornful and threatening. Obviously, they were stronger and more numerous. Each group went its way, Micah in sorrow and frustration, the Danites in triumph (v. 26).

The Danites fell on the peaceful, unsuspecting residents of Laish and exterminated them. They burned the city to the ground. Then they built a new city from scratch and named it Dan. They also built a new sanctuary for Micah's stolen sacred objects and priest. It became a famous religious center in Israel. In fact, verse 30 identifies the young Levite by name and calls him the son of Gershom, who was the son of Moses. In other words, the Danite priesthood claimed descent directly from Moses and was authentically Levitical.

Obviously the writer of Judges had a different view. The altar of Dan was corrupt from the beginning. It was built from stolen and cursed money and shot through with idolatry. This was true long before Jeroboam I established shrines at Dan and Bethel.

The reference to Shiloh (v. 31) is open to several interpretations. It may refer to the Philistine destruction of Shiloh around 1050 BC., the centralization of worship in Jerusalem under David and Solomon, or the destruction of Shiloh by the Assyrians in about 734 BC. The mention of captivity (v. 30) certainly refers to this latter period.

The War with Benjamin (19:1 to 21:25)

The final story in Judges is curious, disturbing, and pathetic. It is hard for us to know what to make of it. Note especially the large number of references to Saul. He was a native of Gibeah in Benjamin, where the original outrage was committed. He was Israel's first king (see 19:1). He was closely associated with Jabesh-gilead (21:8-12), on whose behalf he dismembered the oxen, as the Levite did the body of his concubine.

Beyond that, the dominant point of the story is the anarchy and lawlessness of this period with no centralized national leadership. This situation provided a large measure of the impulse for the establishment of the monarchy.

The Death of the Levite's Concubine (19:1-30)

This chapter concerns a Levite who was connected with Bethlehem and the hill country of Ephraim. His concubine left him. The Revised Standard Version states that she became angry with him, but the footnote mentions the charge of unfaithfulness to her husband, as based on the Hebrew text. With her marriage relationship all but terminated, she took the only course open to her. She returned to her father's house in Bethlehem in Judah.

Four months later her husband went to Bethlehem to try to work out a reconciliation. He was received with hospitality, accomplished his purpose, and extended his stay. The restoration of the relationship called for a celebration. Their return northward was delayed by the father's reluctance to let them depart. It was the fifth day before they finally got away. The father wanted them to stay even longer (vv. 4-9).

The next part of the story indicates that they left Bethlehem three hours before sunset (vv. 9,14). Jebus, or Jerusalem, was five miles north of Bethlehem, about a two-hour journey. Gibeah was four miles and Ramah six miles still further north. It was late when the party reached Jerusalem. The servant wanted to spend the night there, but it was still a Canaanite city, and the Levite decided against it. He wanted to go on to where they could stay with their own people.

Gibeah, in the territory of Benjamin, was an Israelite island surrounded by Canaanite settlements. The group reached the town just as the sun set. They sat down in the open square of the city, just inside the city gate. This area was where all social and business affairs were conducted. The party needed lodging, but they suffered the embarrassment of being completely ignored by the citizens (vv. 14-15). They had ample supplies, but still no one was willing to take them in (v. 19).

Finally an old man from the hill country of Ephraim saw them as he was on his way home from work. He showed them the customary hospitality. He himself was a stranger in Gibeah. He found out something about them and invited them home with him. His words to them included an ominous note of warning. He spoke of danger inherent in staying out in the open (v. 20).

As they were enjoying the old man's hospitality, a depraved group of Gibeah residents suddenly developed an interest in the visitors. They surrounded the house and beat on the door. They demanded that the Levite be sent out to satisfy their homosexual desires (v. 22). The old man tried to talk the rabble out of such perversion. He offered them his own virgin daughter and the Levite's concubine instead.

The men refused to pay any attention to him. Finally the Levite did surrender his concubine to them, in an effort to save his own life. They abused her throughout the night and released her only as dawn broke. She made her way back to the house and collapsed on the threshold, where she died.

Many commentators feel that this outrage of Gibeah was the sin condemned by the later prophet Hosea (9:9; 10:9). As for the homosexuality, it was likely adopted from the Canaanites, who practiced it, especially during times of festival.

A word needs to be said here about the treatment of the woman in this story. The Hebrew world was very much a man's world. Women were regarded as possessions. They were neither equals nor companions. Women and children lived entirely in the personal orbits of men.

When the Levite was about to resume his journey the next morning, he found the concubine dead at the door, with her hands on the threshold. He carried her corpse home. He was angry, not because of any concern for her, but because his dignity and property rights had been violated.

When he reached home he cut the body into twelve pieces, which he sent throughout Israelite territory. This gory act was designed to rally the tribes.

The implication was that they must help him take revenge or else they would suffer the same fate. King Saul later summoned the Israelites to do battle against the Ammonites by doing the same with oxen (1 Sam. 11:6-7).

The concluding verse of the chapter carries these ideas: Did anything like this ever happen before? Consider what it means and get ready to do something about it. As we will soon see, what the Levite did electrified the social conscience of the tribes and summoned them to quick, significant action.

The Punishment of Benjamin (20:1-48)

The Israelites gathered at Mizpah in response to the Levite's gruesome summons. Mizpah was an ancient religious center in the territory of Benjamin, four and one-half miles northwest of Jerusalem and three miles west of Gibeah. Verses 18 and 26 indicate that the headquarters for the campaign were soon moved to Bethel.

There was a general Israelite response. "From Dan to Beersheba" refers to the northern and southern limits of the land. Even Gilead on the eastern side of the Jordan was included, but not Jabesh-gilead (21:8). The Levite reported to this assembly what had happened. He said that he had dismembered his concubine's corpse in order to precipitate such an inquest. He also said that he had surrendered her to the rabble at Gibeah because they intended to kill him. He appealed for counsel (vv. 4-7).

The assembly of tribal leaders and people made a prompt, decisive response. Its members were immediately indignant. There was a unanimous commitment to an expedition of punishment, with the vow that no one would return home until it was accomplished. Arrangements were even made to select 10 percent of their number to arrange for provisions. It was also decided to use the casting of lots to determine who would lead the attack (vv. 8-11).

Before the death sentence was exacted, Israel issued an ultimatum to Benjamin to hand the perpetrators over for execution. The evil had to be eliminated from Israel, just as it had been in the case of Achan (Josh. 7). The Benjamites refused to pay any heed and instead prepared for war (vv. 12-14).

The men of Benjamin were remarkable soldiers. They were skilled in the use of bow and slingshot (1 Chron. 12:1-2). An unusual number of them were left-handed—the term is used only here (v. 16) and of Ehud in 3:15. The Benjamites' overall military skill and the unusual skill of the select troops kept them from worrying about the fact that they were seriously outnumbered.

Before the initial engagement Israel inquired of God at Bethel as to who should go first into battle. As usual, Judah took the lead (see 1:1-2). But the first encounter was a stunning reversal. Israel was severely crippled, and it must have been with difficulty that they were able to re-form and maintain their battle lines (vv. 18-22).

Bethel was seven miles from the battle site. We can picture a large number of the leaders and troops going there, performing acts of contrition, engaging in soul-searching, and seeking the reason for the defeat in this holy war. This second time the question put to the Lord was not who should lead the battle but whether they should attack at all. The answer was affirmative (v. 23).

The second encounter was almost as great a disaster as the first. Again there were substantial losses. This time more of the people went to Bethel, with an even greater degree of earnestness. They waited before the Lord, fasted, and offered burnt offerings and peace offerings (vv. 24-27).

Shiloh was the primary religious center for Israel at this time (see 21:13). However, Bethel was also an ancient religious site. The next verses indicate that the priest and even the ark of the covenant had been temporarily transferred there. This is the only mention of the ark in Judges.

This priest was a descendant of Aaron and even had the name Phinehas that was so highly regarded in that family. Scholars differ as to whether this was the Phinehas we know from Numbers 25:1-8; 31:6 and Joshua 22:13-23 as verse 28 seems to indicate, or a later Phinehas named for his notable ancestor. Phinehas, Aaron's grandson, was a rigid follower of the Lord who was involved in the investigation of the motives of the two and one-half tribes of eastern Palestine.

The third message of the Lord was more definite than the previous ones. Yes, they were to go up. They were assured of victory. This time Israel took a page from Joshua's tactics at Ai (Josh. 8:10-22). They deliberately fell back before the Benjamite counterattack and drew the defenders away from the fortifications of the city. Then they closed the ambush (vv. 29-36).

Verses 36b-44 seem to be a second account of the same final defeat. It gives us more specific details and has a more practical cast. As the Israelites deliberately retreated, some of their forces attacked the defenseless city. The smoke from the burning city was the signal for the retreating forces to move to the attack. The men of Benjamin knew they were beaten and their city lost. They fled in wild disorder to the eastern hills of the wilderness area. Numbers were cut down on the way.

A small remnant of six hundred men was able to escape. Rimmon is five miles northeast of Gibeah. There the Benjamite stragglers eluded Israelite capture for four months before the chase was abandoned. Meanwhile, the bulk of the Israelite force turned back to destroy more accessible targets. People, animals, and cities fell before their destructive wrath.

The Plans for the Survival of Benjamin (21:1-25)

During the muster at Mizpah the other tribes had vowed to refrain from allowing their daughters to marry the men of Benjamin (vv. 1,7,18). However, Benjamin had suffered such incredible losses that the tribe became endangered with extinction (v. 17). With the struggle over, the other tribes began to feel differently about the situation. Their consciences began to bother them. They felt that they had to provide wives for the remaining six hundred refugees or the tribe would become extinct. However, they also had to keep their vow (vv. 6-7).

The people gathered at Bethel (see 20:18,26) to seek a way out of their dilemma. They waited before the Lord, fasted, wept, prayed, and made lamentations. On the second day they built an altar and offered burnt offerings and peace offerings.

Then they remembered that those who had not participated in the campaign against Benjamin were under the curse of death (v. 5). Jabesh-gilead was closely associated with Benjamin and had not participated in the campaign of punishment. Thus Israel sent out a force of twelve thousand crack troops with the dual purposes of punishing the dissenting city by destroying its inhabitants and securing wives for the remnant of Benjamin. In this way four hundred virgins were obtained as brides.

The four hundred brides were returned to Shiloh. Then the people granted unconditional amnesty to the six hundred remaining Benjamites. There was still general sympathy for the group and a desire to restore relationships between the tribes. The people felt a continuing responsibility and, obviously, there was a need for additional brides (vv. 13-18).

That was when someone thought of the annual festival coming up at Shiloh, situated off the main highway from Bethel to Shechem, on the border between Benjamin and Judah. In the book of Joshua, Shiloh was the site of the tabernacle. It was the key Israelite sanctuary in the central highlands before it was destroyed by the Philistines around 1050 BC.

Shiloh was also the site of a yearly festival having to do with the grape harvest. The young ladies of Shiloh participated in a processional dance through the vineyards. Each Benjamite refugee who remained unmarried was instructed to be ready to seize a wife from among the dancing maidens.

This yearly Sadie Hawkins Day in reverse solved the problem but did not technically violate the oath of Mizpah. The brides were taken by their prospective husbands, not given by their fathers. In addition, they were not taken in battle and no life was lost (vv. 19-22).

When the families of any of the girls objected, the leaders of Israel spoke to them about allowing the wives to remain with their new husbands. In this way the plan was carried out, and Benjamin was saved. The men of the tribe went back home to rebuild their cities and restore their land. The tribe had been rehabilitated. However, it was never strong after this time.

And so ends the record of the time of the judges. We are not able to imagine a more exuberant and turbulent period. It was a time when many people were at their worst (v. 25), and some were at their best. It was also a time when the Lord was at work.

RUTH

Introduction

The book of Ruth is easily one of the most familiar and popular in the Bible. It is a charming short story and a perfect example of simple narrative. It would be instructive to check it by contemporary guidelines for writing short stories. Ruth has been compared with the story of Joseph in literary quality. It is a story with a happy ending. There are heroines and a hero but no villain. There is love and suspense. There is tragedy, but it is overcome by courage, love, and loyalty.

Use in Public Worship

Ruth is located in the section of the Hebrew Old Testament called the Writings. It was one of five scrolls grouped together and associated with five religious festivals. Ruth usually was listed second among the five, but sometimes first.

Ruth was read publicly each year during the Feast of Weeks (Pentecost), the second of the annual holy seasons. This harvest festival also celebrated the anniversary of the giving of the covenant at Mount Sinai. The Jewish teachers spoke of the time when the Torah (Law) was given.

Setting, Date, and Purpose

The introductory matters relating to this book are perplexing and largely beyond solution. Fortunately, they affect our appreciation of the book to only a small degree.

Date of contents.—The setting for the book of Ruth is obviously the period of the judges. The book clearly reflects the conditions and customs of that tumultuous time. This is the reason the book is located where it is in our English Bibles. It is supplementary to the book of Judges which precedes it and introductory to the books of Samuel which follow.

Date of writing.—Ruth has been dated all the way from the beginning of the monarchy to the third century BC. Even a casual reading of the book indicates that it cannot have been written before the time of David. He is mentioned by name in 4:22. Chapter 4, verse 7 explains a custom once followed but long since abandoned, and the first verse of the book seems to look back on a time long past.

There are several indications of an earlier date for the book, but most modern scholars feel that evidence for a postexilic time is stronger. Most mention the late fifth or fourth century. This would be during or after the time of Nehemiah and Ezra.

Authorship.—The Jewish Talmud designates Samuel as the author of Ruth, but offers no supporting evidence. We do not know who wrote Ruth.

Purpose.—Disagreement over the purpose of the book is as broad as that over the date of its writing. The least likely view is that it was written to support the practice of levirate marriage. According to that custom a brother-in-law would marry his dead brother's widow and raise up children in the name of the deceased. In Ruth the nearer male relatives are called on to perform this function.

A popular theory is that Ruth was written as a polemic in favor of marriages with foreigners, such as those opposed so bitterly by Nehemiah and Ezra. The book does mention nine times that Ruth was a foreigner. According to this view, the book opposes the viewpoints of such passages as Deuteronomy 23:3; Ezra 9:1 to 10:5; and Nehemiah 13:23-27, while agreeing with such passages as Genesis 1:1-4; 32:2, and 41:45.

However, though Ruth does strike a telling blow for a universal outlook, it does not have any of the characteristics of a polemic. Besides, Ruth was a proselyte who accepted the faith and customs of the Lord's people. She was no longer a foreigner.

The book of Ruth does show the shallowness and selfishness of Jewish particularism. It definitely teaches that the true people of God are any who choose to follow him, not the members of a certain nation or group. The book of Ruth definitely breathes the same spirit as the story of Jonah. It conveys the same outlook as Isaiah 56:6-8. The Lord's grace and care are not limited by national or racial boundaries.

There is no question about the strong note of universalism in Israel's faith. As Ruth shows, even a Moabitess could share in that faith and share in it in a significant way. This is a truth so often emphasized in the New Testament. However, as we reread Ruth we wonder whether, even in our day, we have come up to the level of the Old Testament, much less the level of Jesus.

It may well be that the primary purpose of this book is to tell something about the ancestry of King David. It preserves the tradition that his royal line included Moabite stock. The reader will note that the book ends abruptly as soon as it mentions the name of David.

Other Lessons from the Book of Ruth

This ancient account accents courage and unselfish devotion. It stresses both family and community loyalty. Naomi thought first of the welfare of her daughters-in-law. She always acted with their best interests in mind. Boaz was noble. Ruth was loyal. No wonder this is one of the most popular stories of all time.

This simple narrative also amply illustrates the Lord's providential care. He is clearly at work in the lives of those open to him. This is true even of the members of an obscure migrant family. They suffered repeated tragedy, but where tragedy abounded God's grace much more abounded.

Repeated Tragedy
1:1-22

We can always learn important lessons about ourselves and others when we study how we react to tragedy, particularly tragedy that is repeated and intense. The first chapter of the book of Ruth is a story of tragedy of that nature.

Bereavement in Moab 1:1-18

It is possible to look at the book of Ruth from the standpoint of six separate scenes distinguished by their geographical locations. The opening scene of the book takes place in the land of Moab.

Moab is the high country east of the Dead Sea in what we call Transjordan. It lies south of the Arnon River. It is a dry but fertile area with large grain fields. In fact, the expression "country of Moab" (vv. 1-2) literally means "fields of Moab."

Sometime near the close of the period of the judges, a famine in Israel caused a Hebrew family to migrate to Moab. Such famines were all too common in that area in those times. Both Abraham and Jacob had sought refuge in Egypt during similar famines (Gen. 12:10; 47:4).

The name of the father of the family, Elimelech, means "God is king." His wife's name, Naomi, has the idea of pleasant or agreeable and may mean "my joy" or "my pleasant one." The names of the sons and their wives are much more obscure and much less instructive. The family's intention was to stay in the foreign area only temporarily, for the duration of the emergency. By assuming the role of sojourners, however, the Ephrathites (Bethlehem was also called Ephrathah) forfeited all legal rights. They were much more restricted than our resident aliens here in America who have to register at the local post office each January.

The decade that began with difficulty continued with tragedy. Elimelech died, probably not long after the family's arrival. He left a migrant widow with two sons. The bright part of the story is that the two boys married Moabite girls. However, before the decade in Moab ended both of Naomi's sons died.

In ancient times a childless widow was an unfortunate figure. There was little provision for a widow under the best of circumstances. She is usually mentioned in the same breath with the orphan and the foreigner. With her sons gone, Naomi had to take steps to ensure her own survival. When she learned that the famine was over in Israel, she decided to return home. The three widows set out together on the fifty to sixty mile return trip to Bethlehem (vv. 6-7).

But Naomi thought better of what they were doing. The two daughters-in-law were obviously ready to turn their backs on their homeland. However, Naomi decided that it would be in the girls' best interest if they returned to their homes, not hers. She urged each to return to her mother's tent. This was the common bedouin practice. Naomi also asked for the Lord's blessings on them. For the Lord to deal kindly suggested his unfailing goodness, in fact, goodness beyond what would be expected or strictly required. The measure of their loyalty to her was to be the measure of his graciousness to them. She even wished for each of them a new husband and the security of a happy home (vv. 8-9).

When Naomi kissed the girls good-bye they again showed their true feelings for her by crying aloud and weeping. Her pleas to them to turn back produced the opposite response. They refused to return; instead, they persisted in their determination to accompany her (v. 10).

Naomi pleaded again, this time with more effect. She reminded them that widows without children were wholly dependent on the kindnesses of their relatives. She again urged them to turn back on the basis that their only hope for remarriage would be among their own kin. There would be no hope for levirate marriage if they remained with her. She was widowed herself, and old. She would have no more sons who could take them to wife, and even if she did, the daughters-in-law could not wait until such sons reached marriageable age (vv. 11-13).

Naomi used the term "bitter" (v. 13) to describe the way she felt about the girls' unfortunate lot. She always did have their best interests at heart. That was when Orpah kissed Naomi good-bye and departed. Ruth, however, was more persistent in her loyalty. She vowed to continue to follow Naomi even though her own parents were still alive (see 2:11).

Naomi called Ruth's attention to Orpah's example. She referred to the common belief that leaving one's homeland also meant leaving one's god. Land, god, and people were closely tied together in everyone's mind. But in an incredibly beautiful expression that is certainly the high point of this book, Ruth pledged her love and loyalty to her mother-in-law.

Ruth gently asked Naomi to cease trying to talk her out of what she intended to do. She affirmed that Naomi's home, people, God, and tomb would be hers. The two of them would not be separated either in life or in death. By this expression of personal devotion Ruth convinced Naomi of her devotion and her willingness to forsake her Moabite heritage to live the rest of her life in a foreign land.

In verse 17 Ruth used the personal name for God, translated "the Lord" in most modern versions. It is an indication of the depth of her commitment to the one true God. It was a choice that changed her life and brought her untold blessings. Ruth's choice eventually put her in the royal line of David and had a notable impact on the history of the world.

Return to Bethlehem (1:19-22)

The second scene of the book took place on the western side of the Jordan River, in Bethlehem. Bethlehem lies some six miles south of Jerusalem on the central ridge of Judah. The name means "house of bread" and designates a village situated in the grain fields. It is surrounded by fertile fields of barley and wheat. From Bethlehem Ruth could see the steep slopes of the hill country of Moab to the east, across the Dead Sea.

The appearance of the two women caused a considerable stir in town. The Hebrew words indicate a hum or buzz of conversation and interest. Rumors flew, and probably gossip. We can imagine how quickly the news got around.

"Is this Naomi?" (v. 19) was, of course, a rhetorical question. Some feel it implied condemnation of this one who had forsaken the Lord and gone to the land of Chemosh, the god of the Moabites. This is probably too harsh an understanding of its import. As for Naomi, she shouldered the full weight of her burden. She asked those around her to call her not Naomi (pleasant) but Mara (bitter). The Almighty had dealt bitterly with her. Her lot had been an exceedingly bitter one. We know that throughout Scripture a change of name indicates a change of status. She had left Bethlehem a happy woman, but she had returned empty (vv. 20-21).

So the childless widow with her childless, widowed daughter-in-law— who was also a foreigner—made their home in Bethlehem. Once again the record injects a bright element into an otherwise gloomy picture. Through God's providence they had returned at the best possible time. It was the spring of the year, late April or early May, and the time of the barley harvest (v. 22). Food was plentiful. God was at work in ways not yet evident.

At Work in the Harvest Fields
2:1-23

The third scene in our romantic drama takes place in a barley field near Bethlehem. The grain harvest was under way. This chapter introduces the only other major character in the account. Whereas Naomi was the chief figure of chapter 1, the chief figure here is clearly Boaz.

Ruth in Boaz's Field (2:1-7)

Boaz was an important man in the community. He was a man of wealth and influence. The terms used to describe him came to mean "honorable" and "distinguished." His greeting to his workers (v. 4) indicates his devotion to the Lord and reminds us of Judges 6:12.

Ruth went to glean in Boaz's fields. She did so on her own initiative. She suggested it to Naomi (v. 2). She showed herself willing to work, and she and Naomi were certainly in need. This is how Ruth became their primary source of support.

To glean was to gather the grain that had been dropped or overlooked by the harvesters. This was allowed as a provision for needy strangers, orphans, and widows. In fact, the law forbade the workers from harvesting the fields too closely (Lev. 19:9-10; 23:22; Deut. 24:19-22).

Verse 3 speaks in terms of what we call a chance happening or coincidence. However, the providence of God is clearly in the background of the story. Perhaps the basic lesson this chapter teaches is to trust in the Lord and work hard.

When Boaz arrived on the scene, he noticed and inquired about the stranger. The servant in charge of the reapers had already been impressed with her. She had asked for permission to glean since she, as a foreigner, could not claim such a privilege as a right. She had been working continu-

ously since early morning without even a break. The man also knew and
reported her identity (vv. 6-7).

Boaz's Kindnesses to Ruth (2:8-16)

Boaz already knew about Ruth's devotion to Naomi (v. 11). He also
knew that she had put her trust in the Lord. He made reference to the
Lord's sheltering her under his wings (v. 12; the word can also refer to a
robe or skirt). He was obviously impressed with her, too. He granted to her
several privileges and made special provision for her comfort and safety.

Boaz spoke kindly to her. First of all he insisted that she stay in his fields
and not go elsewhere to glean. He put her with his maidens who gathered
the stalks the men had cut, tied them in bundles, and carried them to the
threshing floor (v. 8).

Boaz also ordered his workers to show respect to Ruth. Laborers such as
these could be crude in speech and in action. A foreigner, in particular,
might be heckled or otherwise molested. The reapers would shout at the
gleaners if they got too close. The gleaners would often have to wait for
some signal from the reapers before they could begin their work. Sometimes
the workmen would ridicule those who were so unfortunate. However,
Boaz warned the young men about bothering Ruth or saying anything to
embarrass her (vv. 9,15).

Boaz provided for Ruth's physical needs by giving her permission to drink
from the large jars of water that had been brought to the fields to refresh the
reapers. No wonder she was so surprised and grateful at being treated so
well! Boaz was treating her like an Israelite or even a member of his own
work force. He was showing her unusual favor and encouragement (vv.
10,13). The fact is that Boaz not only asked for the Lord's blessings on her,
he was also willing to be used of the Lord to answer his own prayer (v. 12).

When the lunch break came, Boaz invited Ruth to share the food and
drink of the reapers. They gathered under some shade or shelter to snack on
pieces of thin, flat bread dipped in sour wine. The taste must have been
something like some of our modern salad dressings. They also ate fresh
heads of grain that had been lightly roasted. In all, it was more than enough.

Ruth's Report to Naomi (2:17-23)

Because of all of Boaz's kindnesses to her (see v. 16), Ruth had a productive day of work. The ephah of barley she threshed out when she finished
gleaning has been estimated from half a bushel to over a bushel. Back at

home she showed Naomi the results of her labors, shared some of the parched grain from lunch, and reported about the day's events (vv. 17-18,21).

It was then that Naomi learned that Ruth had gleaned in Boaz's field, and Ruth learned that Boaz was one of their nearest relatives. Naomi had blessed the generous man before she even knew his name (v. 19), and when she learned his identity she blessed the Lord (v. 20). Boaz's kindnesses proved that the Lord had not forsaken them.

Naomi's reference to the dead (v. 20) indicates that the idea was already in her mind that Boaz might be the one to solve the problem of preserving the name of the dead. The expression "nearest kin" (v. 20) is the Hebrew word *go'el,* often translated "redeemer." It carries the idea of protector or vindicator. It designated the one obligated to look after the weaker members of the family.

The responsibility of the *go'el* involved both name and property. He redeemed the name of the dead through levirate marriage. He redeemed the property of a poor relative by purchasing it and keeping it in the family (Lev. 25:25). He could also be the avenger of blood, according to Numbers 35:12,19-21. This title is used of the Lord as Redeemer in Psalm 19:14; 78:35; Job 19:25; and Isaiah 41:14; 43:14; 44:6; 47:4; 48:17; 49:7. The verb form of this term is used of the Lord in Exodus 6:6; Psalm 106:10; Isaiah 43:1; 44:22-23; 52:9.

So the stage was set for later rapid developments. Ruth worked, unmolested, in Boaz's fields through the wheat harvest, which began two to four weeks later than the barley harvest (vv. 22-23).

Ruth's Appeal to Boaz
3:1-18

The pace of the story quickens considerably as the scene shifts to a threshing floor near Bethlehem. The initiative came from the two women, but the necessary and definite response came from Boaz.

Naomi's Instructions to Ruth (3:1-5)

Once again Naomi gave expression to the responsibility she felt for Ruth's welfare, and, as in 1:9, she had in mind the security of marriage. In that culture, of course, parents arranged the marriages of their children.

It is obvious that Naomi felt that the *go'el*, Boaz, needed to be alerted to his responsibility. She made plans to do just that. Her proposal and Ruth's subsequent actions seem brash and forward to us today; they were probably less so in the time of the judges. It may also be true that social patterns were more relaxed toward the end of the barley harvest. Besides, Ruth had gleaned successfully in the field of this kind man, he was a near relative, and he had shown a definite interest in the Moabite widow.

The winnowing mentioned in verse 2 was the completion of the harvest. The sheaves were untied and the grain spread out in a circle on the hard, smooth surface of the threshing floor. The heads of grain were crushed by the feet of oxen or by a threshing sled or roller studded with sharp pieces of stone and metal. The crushed heads were thrown into the air with a winnowing shovel or fork. The wind blew the loose chaff away. The heavier grain fell into a heap at the worker's feet.

This work of winnowing was done in the evening, to take advantage of the cool breezes coming in off the Mediterranean. The period between four or five o'clock and sunset was usually set aside for this activity. Next came the feasting and drinking appropriate for such a happy occasion. The workers then slept at the threshing floor to protect the grain. The threshing floor itself was usually a large flat rock. This one may have been a community site, but more probably belonged to Boaz and was on his property.

Naomi instructed Ruth to wash and anoint herself and put on her best clothes, perhaps a loose outer garment or a large mantle. Some people feel she was even preparing herself as a bride. She was to wait until after Boaz had eaten and fallen asleep. Then she was to uncover his feet and lie there (vv. 3-4).

Ruth and Boaz at the Threshing Floor (3:6-13)

Ruth willingly carried out Naomi's instructions (vv. 5-7). At midnight Boaz woke up enough to become aware of her presence. His question, "Who are you?" (v. 9), was a startled demand for identification and explanation. Ruth identified herself with an expression of humility and respect.

Her plea was that he spread the skirt of his robe over her because he was the next of kin. This act of covering someone with the skirt symbolized protection. It was especially associated with marriage. See the comments on 2:12, where Boaz used this same symbol of Ruth's relationship with the Lord.

Boaz was greatly impressed with Ruth's attitude. He was a somewhat older man. He noted that she was free to choose a younger man, or one outside the family. Instead she had chosen him, and had chosen to marry within the family of Elimelech. He referred again to Ruth's loyalty and faithfulness to Naomi, matched by even greater devotion and love for him (v. 10).

Boaz was willing to assume his responsibility as next of kin. He also gave Ruth high commendation for her character. He noted that the responsible citizens of the community who gathered in the square inside the city gate knew her to be a worthy woman (v. 11).

However, the fly in the ointment was that there was an even nearer relative who had to be considered. Boaz kept Ruth in safety for the rest of the night and promised that the next morning he would begin the process of assuming the role as kinsman redeemer (vv. 12-13). We wonder if Naomi did not know about the nearer kinsman, or had completely forgotten about him in her excitement.

Ruth's Return to Naomi (3:14-18)

The next morning Ruth got up before daybreak. Boaz cautioned his servants to keep her visit a secret. He indicated his feelings and sealed his vow to her with a gift of barley, perhaps as much as one and one-third bushels (vv. 14-15).

The brief account of verses 16-18 adequately conveys the excitement as Ruth reported to her anxious mother-in-law. We can sense the breathlessness of their hurried conversation. Naomi, when she had been brought up-to-date, was confident that they had done the right thing and that the situation would work out well. She counseled Ruth to have patience, but even readers coming to the chapter's end can feel suspense and excitement about what shortly transpired.

Boaz' Marriage to Ruth
4:1-22

The stage has been amply set for the final chapter of Ruth. It provides a happy conclusion to the record, including solutions to all of the problems.

The Refusal of the Next of Kin (4:1-6)

The next morning after the encounter at the threshing floor Boaz began to act as he had promised. He went up the ridge to the village of Bethlehem. There, within the thick wall with its protective tower, just inside the city gate where the market was set up, was the regular gathering place. All the business of the village was decided in this square. There the elders of the community assembled as a matter of course, to discuss, advise, and decide.

Soon the next of kin to Elimelech and Mahlon came by. He is never identified by name. The Hebrew carries the idea of Mr. So-and-So. Boaz also enlisted ten elders to give their counsel and serve as witnesses to what was at hand (vv. 1-2).

Boaz called everyone's attention to the fact that Naomi was interested in the sale of a plot of land that had belonged to Elimelech. This is despite the fact that one Old Testament passage seems to forbid a widow's controlling family land (Num. 27:8-11). Perhaps Naomi had already disposed of the land, but it could be repurchased by a near relative. Perhaps it was only an insignificant plot. It may have been held in some sort of trust.

Boaz challenged the nearer kinsman to redeem Naomi's property. Boaz, of course, indicated his own desire to obtain the land should the relative decline. The fellow evidently considered it a bargain and quickly agreed to the purchase (v. 4).

That was when Boaz began to read the fine print to the relative. He explained that whichever relative acquired the land had to also marry Ruth in the bargain. She was part of a package deal. The verb in verse 5 has the idea of obtaining in regard to Ruth, but not necessarily the idea of purchase. The firstborn son of a union with Ruth would be legally considered the son of the deceased (v. 5). The land in question would go to this son. There would thus be less inheritance for any other sons they might have or any sons the man might already have.

In verse 6 the relative said twice that he could not play the part of the redeemer under the circumstances. Such a function would evidently disrupt his family situation, impair his inheritance, or otherwise disturb his life patterns. He offered to let Boaz take the right of redemption himself.

Boaz Assumed the Right of Redemption (4:7-12)

The nearer relative took off his sandal and handed it to Boaz before all of the witnesses. This antiquated practice symbolized that he was renouncing his right of redemption. The sandal may have indicated the right of possession, in this case the right of the owner to set foot on the land. This custom was no longer current in the time when this book was written, so the author was careful to explain its significance as the ratification of the transaction.

Thus Boaz bought the land for himself and took Ruth as his wife to perpetuate the name of the dead Mahlon. It may be that, if Boaz had no children, their first son would be the legal heir of both the deceased and the actual father.

All those who were assembled at the gate, in both official and unofficial capacities, pronounced their blessings on the happy couple. They asked that Ruth be like Rachel and Leah who, with their handmaidens, produced the ancestors of the twelve tribes of Israel. They prayed for the prosperity and renown of the couple in Bethlehem and in the larger area of Ephrathah around it. They mentioned Perez (v. 12), the son of Tamar, a Canaanite woman who married Judah. She, too, had been a childless widow but had given birth to twins (Gen. 38:27-30).

The Marriage and Its Results (4:13-22)

The final scene in our romantic drama shifts to the new home of Boaz and Ruth. In time she bore him the expected son. The birth of a male child was an occasion for great celebration. It was customary for the women of the village to lead this celebration. Their expressions on this occasion were expressions of praise to a gracious Lord. Contrast their attitude in verses 14-17 with their previous attitude in 1:19.

Verse 15 also includes further commendation of Ruth, whose devotion had made possible the happy occasion. Ruth was of superlative importance to Naomi, more so even than seven sons, which was the ideal number. Job had that many before and also after his trials. Interestingly enough, this is the only place where the Old Testament uses the term "love" to describe the relationship of one woman to another.

Naomi did not formally adopt her grandson, but she certainly did have all of the normal grandmotherly feelings toward him, plus all of the additional emotions connected with her extraordinary deliverance from her former difficulties. The women of the village even thought of the child as Naomi's own (vv. 16-17). They named him Obed, which means "servant." Maybe they were continuing to commemorate Ruth's devoted service to Naomi.

The genealogy of verses 18-22 is similar to one in 1 Chronicles 2:4-15 (see

Matt. 1:2-6; Luke 3:31-33). It is in highlight or summary form. Its point, of course, is the connection of Ruth and Boaz with David, Israel's most celebrated king. The most interesting name on the list is that of Boaz's father, Salmon, who was one of the two spies of Jericho and the husband of the harlot Rahab (Matt. 1:5).

Without a doubt this brief story, with its genealogical conclusion, teaches that the Lord raises up the humble. He uses the weak things of this world to accent his glory. Those born outside the covenant may still share in that covenant by faith. Not one but three foreign women became ancestors of the greatest of Israel's kings, and of an even greater King who was to come.

The Lord is active in the lives of his people. His wisdom and his love rule and overrule. What more can anyone say but "Blessed be the Lord" (v. 14)?